The Spirit-Magick of Abramelin

Aaron Leitch

Copyright(c)2017 C. "Aaron" Leitch
kheph777@yahoo.com

Visit Us at Doc Solomon's Occult Curios
https://docsolomons.co/wp

Introduction

The *Book of Abramelin*, also known as the *Book of the Sacred Magic*, is among the most famous and unique texts of Renaissance occultism. Much like the more common medieval grimores- such as the *Key of Solomon*, the *Goetia*, the *Heptameron* and others.- it discusses the conjuration of infernal spirits for practical concerns like finding treasure, causing love and friendship, sowing discord, curing sickness, etc, etc.. Yet, Abramelin is unique in that it does not also include detailed instructions on how to go about such conjurations. Instead, the primary focus of the book is upon establishing contact and bonding with one's own Holy Guardian Angel. It is this Angel, then, that instructs one in the necessary details for the conjuration and binding of the Princes of Hell and their many servitors:

> "But your angel will already have instructed you how to convoke them, and will have sufficiently impressed it on your heart. [...] This is wherefore he who wisheth to constrain them should be upon his guard, and follow out faithfully from point to point the instructions which his guardian angel will have given him, and that he impresseth them well upon his memory following them from point to point. [...]

Observing then the doctrine that your angel will have given unto you, and persevering in placing all your trust in God, at length they will appear in the form commanded upon the terrace, upon the sand; when, according to the advice and doctrine received from your holy angel ... you shall propound your demand, and you shall receive from them their oath." -
[*The Book of the Sacred Magic of Abramelin the Mage*, Book II, Ch. 14: "Concerning the Convocation of the Spirits"]

Once the Abramelin aspirant has established contact with his Guardian Angel and learned how to bind the infernal spirits, the text goes on to provide a long list of demons to conjure as well as an entire book of Talismans to use in commanding them.

At first glance, this final portion of the Abramelin system seems incomplete. Very little is left obscure in the invocation of the Guardian Angel, while the end of the book seems to dump the spirit-names and Talismans upon the reader with little beyond the promise of more instruction from the Angel. Because of this, many scholars (myself included, for a time) have jumped to the conclusion that the spirit-magick of Abramelin was an afterthought for the author, or even a much later addition to the manuscript.

However, after a years-long (and on-going) effort to understand Abramelin's system of magick, I no longer suspect this material was an afterthought or later inclusion. In fact, I have discovered a rather sophisticated system of spirit-magick encoded into the existing text. It has simply been written in such a way as to obscure it from the curious, and from those who would attempt to use the Talismans without first making contact with the Guardian Angel.

There is plenty of material available that analyses Abramelin's system of gaining Knowledge of and Conversation with the Holy Guardian Angel. However, precious little has been written about the system of spirit-magick one is supposed to utilize *after* completing the Rite. The purpose of this essay is to focus, at last, upon this long-neglected aspect of Abramelin's magickal system.

A Brief Overview of the Book of Abramelin

The author of the *Book of Abramelin*- one Abraham von Worms- claims to have lived during the reign of Emperor Sigismond of Germany (1368-1437 CE), and to have compiled the manuscript toward the end of his life. S. L. Mathers, in his edition of this text, dates the text to the end of the seventeenth or beginning of the eighteenth centuries. However, it must be remembered that Mathers was working from a French recension of the manuscript discovered in the Biblioteca de l'Arsenal of Paris, and not from the original German version. Thus, it is at least possible that the dates given by Abraham in the older German text are nearly accurate.

The contents of the book are divided into four books (or three in the French recension). The first is an autobiography of Abraham. He describes his years of wandering in search of the True and Sacred Wisdom, and his disappointments along the way. He learns several forms of magick, but finds them all lacking, and their practitioners to fall short of their claims. In the last moments before giving up his quest, Abraham meets an Egyptian adept named Abramelin, who agrees to teach Abraham the Sacred Magic.

The second book, in the German version, contains several chapters of spells that rely heavily on Psalmic magick. (Mathers removed this book from his publication.) Some of the same content can be found in the *5th and 6th Books of Moses*, and the entire book is similar to such works as *Use of the Psalms* or even John Hohman's later compilation *The Long Lost Friend*. They are examples of simple folk-magick that utilize Biblical scripture- especially the Psalms- for talismanic inscriptions, incantations, etc. Abraham describes this as the "blended Qabalah", perhaps referring to the blend of Biblical scripture and folk-magick.

The final two books, in both French and German versions,

are composed of the instructions for the Sacred Magick proper, which Abraham copied by hand from Abramelin's original manuscript. The first part describes a heavily involved procedure of purification and invocation, culminating in the appearance of one's Guardian Angel. The purifications take the standard grimoiric forms of seclusion, fasting, cleanliness, and a heavy dose of prayer. However, where most grimoires require anywhere from a few hours to a month of such purification, the German text insists on no less than a year and a half, divided into three sets of six months each. (The French version abbreviates this to six months, divided into three sets of two months each.)

Throughout the process, very little emphasis is placed upon ceremony. One must establish an Oratory (or prayer room), with an Altar, Oil Lamp, Censor and Holy Oil. To begin with, only the daily prayers are necessary. At a later point a white linen Robe is required during the prayers, along with the lighting of the Lamp and Censor. There are no special sigils, exorcisms or incantations associated with any of these furnishings.

At the end of the period of purification, we find the Abramelin Rite itself - a seven day process divided into three parts. First is the Day of Consecration - where everything involved with the Rite is touched with the Holy Oil and blessed. Next are three days during which the aspirant establishes first-contact with the Guardian Angel. This contact is facilitated by a small square plate of silver1 or a seven-sided figure of silver or wax2 that is placed upon the Altar.

The Angel is then in charge of the final three days of the Rite- called the "Convocation of the Evil (or Unredeemed) Spirits." During this period, a number of infernal spirits are conjured- beginning with the twelve Princes of Hell (more on them below)- to bind them to one's will. These lower beings are commanded to deliver an Oath of obedience to the aspirant, as well as the use of spiritual servants for any number of practical tasks.

However, as I stated previously, Abramelin gives very little information in regard to the infernal spirits. A general overview of the evocational process is given (when to call each spirit and what to demand of them). Plus some notes are included on how to write the conjurations, how to treat and answer the spirits, etc- all of which is very common to exorcism manuals of the medieval and renaissance eras. The notes seem to indicate a fairly standard method of spirit evocation- though without the usual sigils and magick circles we might find in the *Goetia* or *Key of Solomon*.

The Abramelin exorcisms do make use of the Oratory instead of a magick circle. (The spirits are summoned to a Terrace outside the prayer room.) It also instructs the aspirant to don the white linen Robe, a silk over-Robe (white, yellow or rose colored), a white silk Girdle, a Crown depicting various Names of God and a Wand made of almond wood. However, beyond these tools and regalia, the details of the evocation are left for the Angel to provide.

The final book is a collection of word-square Talismans, gathered into "chapters" based on what they are intended to accomplish. There are, for example, chapters of Talismans for invisibility, curing sickness, discovering secrets, causing visions, finding treasure and much more. It is upon these mystical word-squares the demonic Princes and spirits must swear when giving their Oaths. Each Talisman can then be used to command a servient spirit to perform a related task.

The Princes of Hell

The Convocation of Unredeemed Spirits is not lightly undertaken. Over a three day period, the aspirant must summon the twelve ruling Princes of Hell - who come in three groups of four. On the first day, the supreme (or sovereign) rulers Lucifer, Leviatan (or Leviathan), Satan and Belial are called. All four of these names appear throughout Judeo-Christian literature and legend, sometimes as different beings and sometimes as different names for the same being - the Fallen Angel who reigns supreme in Hell.3

In the Abramelin system, the aspirant summons all four

names as if they were distinct personalities. Once they have been constrained and their Oaths of loyalty have been obtained, they are commanded to return the next day with the remaining eight sub-Princes.

The first group of sub-Princes is composed of Astarot (or Ashtaroth), Magot, Asmodee (or Admodeus) and Belzebud (or Beelzebub, Beelzeboul). Three of them (exclusive of Magot) are well established in Judeo-Christian literature and legend as powerful rulers in Hell. Both Asmodeus and Beelzeboul are credited with the title "King of Demons" and are often used synonymously with "the Devil" or Satan. The names of Ashtaroth and Beelzeboul are traced to the ancient Palestinian Gods Astarte and Baal Zebul (Lord of the High Place), who were demonized by the authors of the Old Testament. Magot (the "t" is silent), meanwhile, appears to be a French word that either refers to a baboon-like monkey (the Barbary Ape), or to a hoard/stash/nest egg. He may be one and the same with the demon Maguth- who appears in medieval occult literature such as the *Heptameron*.

The second group of sub-Princes is composed of the Demon Princes of the four quarters of the world. These four are found throughout medieval and renaissance occult literature, in various forms. Agrippa lists them as Oriens/Uriens (King of the East), Paymon (King of the West), Egyn/Egin (King of the North) and Amaymon (King of the South). In the *Testament of Solomon* we find them as Oriens, Amemon, Boul and Eltzen. They are known in Rabbinical legend as Azazel, Samael, Azael and Mahazael. In the *Book of Abramelin* they are called Oriens, Paymon, Ariton and Amaimon. They are the most terrestrial of the twelve Princes, and therefore have the most direct influence upon physical events.

I suspect these Princes, grouped into three sets of four, are intended to represent the elemental forces of the zodiac. It is not at all uncommon in demonology to find groups of demons associated with the twelve zodiacal signs. In the *Testament of Solomon*, the sorcerer-king summons the 36 demons of the Decanates, a concept which traces itself back to ancient Chaldea and from there back to Egypt. Medieval texts of necromancy such as the *Goetia* retain much zodiacal imagery in their descriptions of the spirits. Therefore, it would not be surprising at all to find zodiacal associations for the spirits of Abramelin.

The four supreme Princes could easily be associated with the four Fixed Signs, as chthonic counterparts to the four celestaial beasts: thus Lucifer (the Light Bringer) representing Fixed Fire (Leo/Lion), Leviathan (the sea monster) representing Fixed Water (Scorpius/Eagle), Satan (the Accuser) representing Fixed Air (Aquarius/Man) and Belial (the Worthless or He Who Shall Not Rise) representing Fixed Earth (Taurus/Ox). The four Kings of the Quarters are traditionally associated with the

Cardinal Signs (which fall on the four quarters on a zodiacal chart): Oriens in the East (Aries), Paymon in the West (Libra), Ariton in the North (Cancer) and Amaimon in the South (Capricorn). This would leave the remaining four sub-Princes to rule the Mutable Signs of Sagittarius, Gemini, Virgo and Pisces.

Gathering your Servient Spirits

In order to give proper instruction on Abramelin's spirit-magick, it is first necessary to return to the seven-day Abramelin Rite - specifically to the final three days, wherein we find the Convocation of the Unredeemed Spirits. This is where the twelve Princes of Hell are conjured and oaths of loyalty are demanded of them. It is also here that the Princes provide any number of lesser spirits who must serve the aspirant for the rest of his life, and this is what concerns us here.

At some time previous to the Convocation of Unredeemed Spirits, the aspirant is instructed to browse through the Talismans given in the final book and choose those that are most appealing or useful:

> "But the greatest part of the symbols of the third book I counsel you to make before commencing the operation, keeping them until that time in the interior of the altar." - [*The Book of the Sacred Magic of Abramelin the Mage*, Book II, Ch. 20, "How the operations should be performed."]

Originally, I made the mistake of assuming it was necessary to draw out *all* of the Talismans beforehand. However, you only need to choose those that appeal to you the most, and keep in mind that (as we shall see below) more Talismans can be drawn up later as needed.

When gathering the Talismans for your own use, remember that a good number of them in the French recension are incorrect, incomplete or mislabelled. In recent years, Georg Dehn has made the older German manuscripts available to the English speaking world- including a completed set of Talismans. However, even the German originals contain errors that need correction, which I addressed in my essay *Abramelin's Magickal Word Squares* (included in this book). I am sure you will find that essay very useful in your own exploration of Abramelin's magick.

Once you have gathered and penned the Talismans that seem most useful, it is then necessary to browse the long lists of servient spirits found in the next-to-last book (Book II in Mathers' edition, Book III in the Dehn version). From these, you must compile your own list of the spirits you will desire as servitors. However, much as we found with the Talismans, it is not necessary to include *every* spirit name found in Abraham's lists. It is only necessary to gather those which appeal to you personally.

> "It is for you to demand from these [sub-Princes] the other spirits which you may wish to have; but seeing that they be infinite in number, and one more skilful in service than another, one for one matter, another for another; you shall

make a selection of the spirits whom you wish..." - [*The Book of the Sacred Magic of Abramelin the Mage*, Book II, Chapter 15, "Concerning what you should demand of the spirits..."]

"I will here give a very exact description of many spirits, the which (names) either altogether or in part, or else as many of them as you may wish, you should give written upon paper unto the eight sub-princes, on the second day of the conjuration. [...]

Infinite be the spirits which I could have here set down, but in order not to make any confusion, I have thought fit to put only those whom I have myself employed, and whom I have found good and faithful in all the operations wherein I have availed myself of them." - [*The Book of the Sacred Magic of Abramelin the Mage*, Book II, Ch. 19, "A descriptive list of the names of the spirits..."]

Therefore, let us consider the method of choosing the right spirits for you:

Directly following the lists of spirits, Abraham outlines which of the Princes of Hell are responsible for the operation of each chapter of Talismans. Some of these sets are governed by a single sub-Prince, and others are directed by two or more sub-Princes together. (The primary four Princes- Lucifer, Satan, Leviathan and Belial- do not directly govern any of the Talismans.)

Meanwhile, the lists of spirit-names are categorized in the exact same way. There are twelve
groups of spirits indicated, each one governed by one or more Sub-Princes:

1. ASTAROT   **2.** MAGOT   **3.** ASMODEE   **4.** BELZEBUD
5. ASTAROT and ASMODEE   **6.** MAGOT and ASMODEE

7. ORIENS   **8.** PAIMON   **9.** ARITON   **10.** AMAIMON
11. ALL FOUR TOGETHER
12. ARITON and AMAIMON

These twelve groups cover the operations of all of the Talismans given in the book. Therefore, by comparing the Princes who govern these groups to the Princes who govern the various chapters of Talismans, we can determine which spirits must be conjured to work any given operation.

Take for example the first chapter of Talismans- "To know all manner of things past and future"- which are governed collectively by the four sub Princes Oriens, Paymon, Ariton and Amaimon. Consulting the list of spirit-names, we find a relatively large group of servitors governed by the same four sub-Princes. (The following is not a complete list.):

> Moreh, Saraph, Proxonos, Nabhi, Kosem, Peresch, Thirama, Alluph, Neschamah, Milon, Frasis, Chaya, Malach, Malabed, Yparchos, Nudeton, Mebhaer, Bruach, Apollyon, Schaluah, Myrmo, Melamod, Pother, Sched, Eckdulon, Manties, Obedamah, Jachiel, Iuar, Moschel, Pechach, Hasperim, Katsin, Phosphora, Badad, Cohen, Cuschi, Fasma, Pakid, Helel, Marah, Raschear, Nogah, Adon, Erimites, Trapis, Nagid, Ethanim. Patid, Nasi, Parelit, Emfatison, Parasch, Girmil, Tolet, Helmis, Asmiel... [*The Book of Abramelin*, Book III, Ch. 19, "The names of spirits you can call and how to call them."]

Therefore, any of these spirits can be conjured to reveal information about things past and future. All that remains is to decide which of these entities should be demanded from the Princes during the Convocation in order to serve you for the purpose.

First and foremost, look for any spirit names that actually appear on the Talisman you wish to use. For example, the first Talisman in chapter one (to know all things past and future in general) contains the name of the very first spirit given in the list:

Moreh. Therefore, if you wish to use this particular Talisman, it would be best to add *Moreh*'s name to your list.

```
M O R E H
O R I R E
R I N I R
E R I R O
H E R O M
```

Next, consider the possible meanings of the spirit's names in relation to the functions they must perform.4 For example, *Moreh*'s name is Hebrew for "teacher or oracle." In the same group of spirits (see the list of names above) we find *Nabhi*, whose name translates as "prophecy." *Kosem'*s name means "to divine, predict." *Alluph*'s name translates as "to teach, learn" *Melammed* indicates "a teacher of religion or spiritual matters." All of these names are quite well suited for the first chapter of Talismans, to know "all manner of things..."

In this way, you can go about drawing up a preliminary register of spirit-names. This is the very same register you will present, along with your chosen Talismans, to the Princes and sub-Princes during their Convocation.

However, the register you take into the Convocation is not likely the final version you will end up with. According to the

Book of Abramelin, the Princes of Hell will have some input on which spirits are right for you:

> "...and in the first demand which thou shalt make unto the four spirits (who are) the supreme princes, and unto the eight sub-princes; thou shalt demand the most skilful of the spirits, of whom thou shalt make a register for convenience of the practice...
>
> But seeing that the subjects of various erring humours (of mind) and other occasions which arise daily be diverse, each man will procure for himself those (spirits) which be of his nature and genius and fit for that wherein thou wouldest employ them." - [*The Book of the Sacred Magic of Abramelin the Mage*, Book III, "Essential remarks upon the foregoing symbols."]

Therefore, it is not likely you will possess the names of *all* of your servitors before performing the Convocation of Unredeemed Spirits. It will be necessary to ask the Princes, during the Convocation, which spirits are best suited to your personal psychological make-up.

Meanwhile, the Guardian Angel can expand this list any time He or She wishes. I suspect the following quote is intended to refer to the reception of new Talismans *after* the Abramelin Rite is complete (which we shall discuss later):

> "And these (spirits) be not vile, base, and common, but of rank, industrious, and very prompt unto an infinitude of things. Now their names have been manifested and discovered by the angels, and if you should wish for more the angel will augment them for you as far as you shall wish; seeing that their number is infinite." - [*The Book of the Sacred Magic of Abramelin the Mage*, Book III, Chapter 19, "A descriptive list of the names of the spirits..."]

Keep in mind that you may very well receive names that are not found anywhere in the given lists. While you certainly can share some of the same spirits utilized by Abraham, his lists are ultimately personal to him alone. Your spirits may be entirely unique, or (most likely) a mixture of Abraham's and your own.

Because of this, I suggest creating a register of names that can be easily expanded during and after the Convocation itself. The given register of twelve groups appears incomplete to me, as there are several possible combinations of sub-Princes that are not included. For instance, note that Astarot, Magot, Asmodee and Belzebud- while they each have their own headings- have no grouping for the four of them together. Plus, while it is clearly indicated that the two sets of sub-Princes work in pairs, only a small number of possible pairings are included. If we create a more complete register, it would look like this:

1. ASTAROT   2. MAGOT   3. ASMODEE   4. BELZEBUD
5. ALL FOUR TOGETHER
6. ASTAROT and MAGOT   7. ASTAROT and ASMODEE
8. ASTAROT and BELZEBUD
9. MAGOT and ASMODEE   10. MAGOT and BELZEBUD
11. ASMODEE and BELZEBUD

12. ORIENS   13. PAIMON   14. ARITON   15. AMAIMON
16. ALL FOUR TOGETHER
17. ORIENS and PAIMON   18. ORIENS and ARITON
19. ORIENS and AMAIMON   20. PAIMON and ARITON
21. PAIMON and AMAIMON   22. ARITON and AMAIMON

The *Book of Abramelin* does not include any groupings of three Princes at a time, nor does it indicate that the two groups of sub-Princes ever cross-over in pairings. Therefore, my above register follows the same pattern- resulting in eleven groupings for each set of sub-Princes, and twenty-two groups overall.

Depending on which Talismans you choose, you can have spirit names in up to twelve of these groups before beginning the Convocation of Unredeemed Spirits. Then, during the

Convocation, more names can be added to any of the given twenty-two headings by the sub-Princes. This completed (yet still open-ended!) register is presented to the sub-Princes on the second day of the Convocation. After completing the Rite, any number of further names can be added as you put the magick into practice.

Besides these spirits, the aspirant is also instructed to demand the names of four additional Familiars- one granted by each of the "directional" sub-Princes (Oriens, Paymon, Ariton and Amaimon). The four Familiars are linked especially to the Talismans of chapter five, "How we may retain the familiar spirits bond or free in whatsoever form."

These four spirits are set above the others, as they will serve as your direct liaisons with the spirit-world and will act as more general-purpose workers than those included in the register. They remain "on call" at all times, each one taking charge successively depending on the time of day: The Familiar granted by Oriens will be active from dawn to noon. The one granted by Amaimon will act from noon to dusk. The Familiar granted by Paymon will be active from dusk to midnight, and that granted by Ariton will be in charge from midnight until dawn. (These times of day are associated with the direction ruled by each spirit on a zodiacal chart. East = dawn, South = noon, West = dusk and North = midnight.)

While Abramelin suggests we do not use the Talismans with the Four Familiars (except, of course, the Talismans of the fifth chapter) he also lists several operations for which the Familiars might serve instead of the Talismans:

> Chapter 2: Scientific Information
> Chapter 4: Diverse Visions
> Chapter 12: Secrets of Others.
> Chapter 18: Healing
> Chapter 19: Affection and Love
> Chapter 23: Demolishing Buildings
> Chapter 24: Discovery of Theft
> Chapter 27: To Cause Visions
> Chapter 28: Obtaining Money
> Chapter 30: Visions of Operas, Comedies, etc.

I notice that most of these operations are centred around divination or visions of various sorts. Although, their usefulness in demolishing buildings and bringing money suggests more practical applications as well. This is supported in the final book, where further information about working with the Familiars is hidden:

> "The familiar spirits are very prompt, and they are able to

execute in most minute detail all matters of a mechanical nature, with the which therefore it is well to occupy them; as in historical painting; in making statues; clocks; weapons; and other like matters; also in chemistry; and in causing them to carry out commercial and business transactions under the form of other persons; in making them transport merchandise and other goods from one place to another; also to employ them in causing quarrels, fights, homicides, and all kinds of evils, and malefic acts; also to convey letters and messages of all kinds from one country to another; to deliver prisoners; and in a thousand other ways which I have frequently experimented." - [*The Book of the Sacred Magic of Abramelin the Mage*, Book III, "Essential remarks upon the foregoing symbols."]

Thus, we have a fairly clear idea of what uses our Familiar Spirits should have.

Finally, the Convocation of Unredeemed Spirits ends on the third day (which is in fact the last of the seven day Abramelin Rite). The Princes are all called once again, and this time the sub-Princes should appear with all of the requested servient and Familiar spirits. Oaths are sworn to the aspirant once more, but this time they are sworn upon each set of Talismans. The lesser spirits must promise to serve the aspirant without hesitation, and to act whether or not the Talismans themselves are employed.

Using the Magick - Post Abramelin

In fact, the Talismans used during the Convocation are relegated to a position of secondary importance when the magick is put into practice. Abraham explains the system toward the end of Book II (of the Mathers version, or Book III in the Dehn version):

> "You are then to understand that once he who operateth hath the power, it is not necessary to use written symbols, but it may suffice to name aloud the name of the spirit, and the form in which you wish him to appear visibly; because once they have taken oath, this sufficeth. These symbols, then, be made for you to avail yourself of them when you be in the company of other persons; also you must have them upon you, so that in touching or handling them simply, they may represent your wish. Immediately then he unto whom the symbol appertaineth will serve you punctually; but if you should desire something special which is in no way connected with or named in the symbol, it will be necessary to signify the same at least by showing your desire by two or three words. [...]
>
> But when it is a grave and important matter, you should retire into a secret place apart, provided it be appropriate,

for any place is good to invoke the spirits proper unto the operation. There give them their commission regarding that which you wish them to perform, the which they will either execute then or in the days following. But always give them the signal by word of mouth, or in any other manner that may be pleasing unto you, whenever you wish them to begin to operate." [*The Book of the Sacred Magic of Abramelin the Mage*, Book II, Chapter 20, "How the operations should be performed."]

In the same chapter, Abraham provides a long list of rules which the aspirant must observe. Some of them apply to the Rite of Abramelin itself, while others are intended to regulate the use of the magick afterwards. Below, I have included the rules that apply to our current discussion:

> " (1) Take heed before all things to perform no magical operation soever, or invocations of the spirits on the Sabbath day, during the whole period of your life, seeing that that day is consecrated unto God, and is the day on which you should repose and sanctify yourself, and you should solemnise it by prayers.
> (6) In conversing with spirits good or evil, never employ words which you do not understand, because even so will

you have shame and hurt.

(11) If the operations can be performed by the familiar spirits, it is not necessary to employ others therein.

(12) Though it should be an easy matter for you to employ your familiars to annoy your neighbour, seek to abstain therefrom, unless it were to repress the insolence of such as might attempt aught against you personally. Never keep the familiar spirits in idleness, and should you wish to give one over unto any person, see that such person be distinguished and meritorious, for they love not to serve those of base and common condition. But should such person unto whom you give them have made some express pact (with spirits) in such case the familiar spirits will fly in haste to serve him.

(18) You shall not permit the familiar spirits to familiarise themselves too much with you, through your disputing and arguing with them; because they will propound so many affairs and things at once as to confound and trouble the mind.

(19) With the familiar spirits you should not make use of

the symbols of the third book, unless it be those of the fifth chapter thereof; but if you desire anything, command them aloud to perform it. Never commence many operations at once and in the same time, but when you have finished one then begin another, until you are perfect in the practice; for an apprentice artist doth not become a master suddenly, but little by little.

(20) Without reasons of the very last importance, the four princes or the eight sub-princes should never be summoned, because we must make a great distinction between these and the
others (who are inferior to them).

(21) In operating, as rarely as possible insist upon the spirits appearing visibly; and thus you will work all the better, for it should suffice you for them to say and do what you wish.

(22) All prayers, orations, invocations, and conjurations, and in fact everything you have to say, should be pronounced aloud and clearly, without however shouting like a madman, but speaking clearly and naturally, and pronouncing distinctly.

(24) Take heed that you commence no operation at night if it be important, unless the need be very pressing."

[Note: the following instruction appears at the very end of the chapter, and only in the French recension:] Every time that you shall desire to make a fresh command, you shall thrice repeat the Psalm [91], "*Qui habitat in adjutorium Altissimi,*" etc., "Whoso dwelleth in the aid of the Most High," etc. -- because this Psalm possesseth so great a virtue that you will be astonished when you comprehend it.

- [*The Book of the Sacred Magic of Abramelin the Mage*, Book II, Chapter 20, "How the operations should be performed."]

In these rules we find a good overview of the magickal system - telling us where, when and how to perform the spirit-work. You may notice that no mention whatsoever is made of further ceremonies. Once the spirits have been summoned and bound by their Oath, it is not necessary to employ full evocational ceremonies in order to issue new orders to them. (Take special note of rule 21, which dissuades the aspirant from demanding even the visible appearance of the spirits, when speaking their name and issuing the command should suffice.)

However, I must add from my personal experience, that it can be useful to employ the Oratory, Robes and Crown, Wand and Talismans when summoning the spirits- especially in the beginning. The added ceremony helps to facilitate the communication between the aspirant and his spirits while the working relationship is built. Over time, and with diligent practice, the necessity of the extra tools and ceremony should decrease.

Meanwhile, instead of elaborate ceremonies, the *Book of Abramelin* suggests a more folkstyle method of employing the Talismans. This is found at the end the same chapter (20), where Abraham records specific instructions for using several sets of the Talismans. I have included several examples below:

> **Chapter 1.** (To know all manner of things past and future, which be not however directly opposed to God, and to his most holy will.)
>
> First take the symbol in your hand, place it (upon the top of your head) under your hat, and either you will be secretly warned by the spirit, or he will execute that which you have the intention of commanding him to do.

"**Chapter 13.** (To cause a dead body to revive, and perform all the functions which a living person would do, and this during a space of seven years, by means of the spirits.)

Nothing else is necessary than to be attentive to the moment when the man is just dead, and then to place the symbol upon him towards the four quarters of the world; and at once he will lift himself up and begin to move himself he should then be dressed; and a symbol similar to that which hath been placed upon him should be sewn into his garment.

"**Chapter 14.** (The twelve symbols for the twelve hours of the day and of the night, to render oneself invisible unto every person.)

[...] You have in this chapter twelve symbols, for twelve different spirits submitted unto Prince Magot, who are all of the same force. You should put the symbol (upon the top of your head) under the hat or bonnet, and then you will become invisible; while on taking it away, you will appear visible again.

"**Chapter 22.** (This chapter is only for evil, for with the symbols herein we can cast spells, and work every kind of evil; we should not avail ourselves hereof.)

All these symbols are to be either buried in the ground, or placed under doors, steps, or buried under paths and other places by which people do pass, or whereon they lean; in this latter case it is sufficient merely to touch (such places) with the symbol."

[*The Book of the Sacred Magic of Abramelin the Mage*, Book II, Ch. 20, "Instructions and explanations concerning what points we should particularly observe..."]

There is a certain ring of similarity between this kind of magick and what is contained in Book II of the German version, the so-called "Blended Qabalah." I also find two further important points inferred by these instructions:

One: They support the idea that the Talismans used during the Convocation of Unredeemed Spirits are not always employed in the magick afterwards. Notice, for example the instructions for Chapter 13, where a copy of the Talisman (apparently made of parchment or cloth) is sewn into the subject's clothing. Or Chapter 22, which requires the symbols to be buried in various places - which I assume does not indicate burying the original Talisman. It would seem that the letters of the symbol (which can be inscribed anywhere) are more important than the actual piece of paper the original is written upon.

Given the folk-style of this kind of magick, Talismans acquired at a later date may also come with instructions that do not involve using the original. For example, some folk healing spells require inscribing a figure with honey inside a bowl, then filling the bowl with milk and having the subject drink it. Some protection spells require engraving a symbol upon a particular substance (such as wax, lead or iron) and then burying or hiding it somewhere. If these are the kinds of instructions one receives for using the Abramelin Talismans, it would be unlikely the originals would be employed for the purpose. And this leads to the second important point:

Two: It appears that each Talisman you acquire while using the magick will come with its own specific instructions- likely given by the Guardian Angel or sub-Prince (whichever one reveals the Talisman). We will discuss the method of acquiring new Talismans next.

Acquiring New Talismans

It is expected that the final book of Abramelin will not contain a Talisman for every need the aspirant will face in a lifetime:

> "Now will I teach you how all those (symbols) which be in this book, as well as those which you will (hereafter) receive from the spirits (themselves), ought to be written down and acquired. For the number of operations is infinite, and it would be an impossibility to set them all down in this work" - [*The Book of the Sacred Magic of Abramelin the Mage*, Book III, "Essential remarks upon the foregoing symbols."]

Therefore, there are methods described in the text for obtaining new squares. In fact, there are two different methods, depending on what kind of magick one wishes to accomplish and (therefore) which spiritual entity will reveal the letters. In Book II (of the Mathers version, or Book III of the Dehn version) Abraham takes the time to categorize all of the Talismans into those revealed by the Guardian Angel, those revealed by the infernal Spirits and those which are a mixture of the two. (See Book II, "By whom the symbols of the third book be manifested.")

It is not readily apparent why Abraham has placed his Talismans in one category or the other. One might expect all Talismans used for good would be revealed by the Angel, and those used for evil would be revealed by the Spirits. However, the divisions suggested by Abraham do not seem to follow such a clear formula. Instead, it seems to have more to do with whether or not permission to use the Talismans was granted or withheld by his Guardian Angel. Thus, the Talismans revealed by the Angel are always permissible. Those revealed by either the Angel or Spirits (or both together) require one to ask permission before each use. Finally, those revealed only by the Spirits still require permission from the Angel before use, but they involve types of magic the Angel would not reveal.

Of course, when you are ready to obtain a new Talisman, you may or may not know beforehand which entity will reveal it. Fortunately, the two methods begin in the same manner, so you can discover which direction to follow as you go along:

1) If you wish to obtain a Talisman from your Guardian Angel, it is best to perform the Rite on the day of the Sabbath. (Sunday if your background is Christian, Saturday if you are Jewish.) However, if you intend to obtain the Talisman from the infernal spirits, any other day will suffice.

2) You will need to set up your Oratory just as you did throughout the Abramelin Rite. You will have the Altar, Censor and Incense, Holy Oil, Lamp and the Plate of Silver (or Wax). You will also need to have the exorcism regalia on hand: the silk over-robe, the Crown, the Girdle and the Almond Wand- in case you need to summon the Spirits. Finally, you will also need clean paper and a pen, and I strongly suggest obtaining a Hebrew lexicon as well. (I will explain the lexicon later.)

3) You must fast the day before the ceremony. The *Book of Abramelin* states that all fasts begin at dusk (or, the "first nocturnal star"), so you will likely only need to fast for about 12 hours before you begin the work. Drink only water during this period.

4) Then, at dawn, clean yourself thoroughly, don the

White Robe and enter the Oratory with the pen, paper and lexicon. Light the Censor and the Lamp, place the Silver (or wax) Lamen on the Altar, then kneel and perform the usual prayers. That is, first pray to the Highest (Adonai Zabaoth) in confession, then in thanksgiving, and then ask Him to send your Guardian Angel to aid you in the matter.

5) Stand and recite Psalm 138 ("I will praise Thee with my whole heart..."). Then, begin to invoke the Angel directly - asking for his/her presence and council concerning your need.

6) If the Guardian Angel never appears nor deigns to speak to you on the subject, then you know that you have not been granted permission to work the desired magick. It is strongly suggested that you break off the attempt, give your prayers of thanks, and leave the Oratory. Then rethink your plan of action and try again at a later date.

7) If the Guardian Angel does appear and speaks with you, he may reveal the Talisman to you himself. If so, you need only write down the letters of the Talisman, along with the name(s) of the spirits who will perform the operations (or that of the sub-Prince who will govern it). Plus, as I stated

previously, you will also be given instructions on how to employ the Talisman in practice.

8) Once complete, make your prayers of thanks, then leave the Oratory just as it is for the rest of the day. At dusk, return to make your evening prayers (as you did during the Abramelin Rite), clean and put away the Silver Plate, and close the Oratory.

On the other hand, if you desire a Talisman from the infernal spirits, you must follow the same procedure up to step four. Then:

5-a) Don the over-Robe, Girdle and Crown, and take up the almond Wand. Recite Psalm 91 ("Whosoever dwelleth in the secret place of the Most High...") three times.

Then, turn toward the Terrace and conjure the Princes as you did during the Convocation. Once they have appeared and been reminded of their Oaths, request the new Talisman from them. The sub-Prince(s) in charge of the operation will reveal the letters of the word-square, along with the name(s) of the spirits who will perform the work. Plus, they will give you special instructions for putting the

Talisman to use.

6-a) Have the sub-Prince(s) that will govern the operation, together with the spirit(s) who will perform the work, swear upon the new Talisman as they did for the others. Then license them to depart, and perfume the area with the Censor.

7-a) The same instructions for closing down the Oratory apply here as in Step 8 above. Leave the Oratory as it is until the evening, when you shall return to make your evening prayers and put everything away.

Abraham also gives us some notes on the materials we need to create the Talismans and how they should be handled afterwards:

> "And remember, that as there is a God to write these aforesaid symbols, there is no particular preparation necessary of pens, of ink, and of paper; nor yet of elections of particular days, nor other things to be observed, which the false magicians and enchanters of the devil would have you believe. It sufficeth that the symbols should be clearly written with any kind of ink and pen,

provided that we may easily discern unto what operation each sign appertaineth, the which also you can easily do by means of a properly arranged and drawn up register of them. [...] And after that the spirits shall have taken oath thereupon, you shall carefully keep (the symbols) in a safe place, where they can neither be seen nor touched by any other person, because thus great harm might befall such person." [*The Book of the Sacred Magic of Abramelin the Mage*, Book II, "How the operations should be performed."]

Just as we have seen elsewhere in this text, the above passage contains an aversion to the methods of the more common grimoires of goetic conjuration. No special considerations must be taken for pens, inks, paper or magickal timing. Yet again it would appear that the letters of the word-squares are what is important, rather than the paper upon which they are drawn.

Creating Word-Squares

In the *Book of Abramelin*, Abraham suggests the Talisman and the name of its spirit will appear "like dew" upon the Silver Plate (when revealed by the Angel) or else scribbled into the sand upon the Terrace (when revealed by the spirits). Personally, I would not expect such a direct physical manifestation. Instead, much of the information will have to be skryed by the aspirant while communicating with the entities. Plus, some of it will require an understanding of how to create word-squares.

Unfortunately, Abraham devotes no time in his instructions to educating the reader on the subject of word-squares. I have addressed this issue in my essay *Abramelin's Magickal Word Squares*. In order to save space, I refer the reader there for my full explanation. Here, I will simply summarize the important points and apply them to Abramelin Talismans. (This is where that lexicon comes into play!)

There are three types of word-squares: First is the Acrostic (or standard word-square), where the words read the same forward and downward. For example:

```
B I T
I C E
T E N
```

The second type- which is very rare among Abraham's Talismans- is the Double Acrostic, where the words read differently forward and downward. For example:

```
T O O
U R N
B E E
```

Finally, the third type of word-square is called the Perfect Double Acrostic, which reads the same forward, backward, downward and upward. Take for example this square from the *Book of Abramelin* (chapter 5, to retain the Familiar spirits in the form of an Eagle):

```
N E S H E R
E L E E H E
S E P P E H
H E P P E S
E H E E L E
R E H S E N
```

The keyword of this square is *Nesher*- Hebrew for "Eagle." Note how *Nesher* and the other words in the square can be read left to right, downward, right to left and upward. Which type of square you create will be largely determined by the words you use to compile it, however the Perfect Double Acrostic seems to be the most common type found in *The Book of Abramelin*.

When it is time for you to construct a new Talisman, you must first ask the Angel or sub-Princes for the keyword of the square. This keyword will be one of two things: either the name of the spirit who will perform the operation, or a word that sums up the desired effect. If it is the name of a spirit who is *not* currently in your register, then I strongly suggest that, after compiling the new Talisman, you continue forward to summon the sub-Princes. Have them bring the new spirit to you and swear an oath of loyalty upon the new Talisman.

Meanwhile, most of Abraham's Talismans contain a keyword that indicates the goal of the operation. For example, the fourth Talisman of chapter four is intended to facilitate visions in jewels or rings. Its keyword is B E D S E R, which is adapted from the Hebrew word *Betzer* (BTzR) meaning "gold or golden ring." In another example, the first Talisman of chapter six is intended to help with mining work, and its key word is S E L A A H, adapted from the Hebrew word *Selah* (SLH) meaning "to lift up." In your own work, you may ask the Angel or sub-Princes to suggest such a keyword and/or to guide you to the necessary word in the Hebrew lexicon. (Other languages can be used as well—such as Latin, Greek, Chaldean, Egyptian, etc, etc.)

Once you have your keyword, the real work begins. Keep

in mind that word-squares are traditionally *puzzles*, so expect to put some real work into this! You will have to discover the size of your word-square (that is, how many cells in the grid), where exactly to place the keyword into the grid and finally several further words that both relate to your magickal goal and fit into the linguistic structure of the square. And none of these are set in stone!

To determine the size of the square, it is first necessary to determine how best to write the keyword. Remember that Hebrew letters do not transliterate directly into English. Therefore, there are no set rules for how a Hebrew word should be spelled when written in English characters. It is most important that the English-adaptation be phonetically similar to the Hebrew original. Take for example the Hebrew word QBLH, which means "Tradition" and can be spelled *Qabalah*, *Cabala* or even *Khabbalah*. These are all the same word, written in different ways by different people at different times.

Therefore, if your keyword can be written with four letters, then your new square will be a 4 x 4 grid. If it must be written with 6 letters, then your square will be 6 x 6, etc. If the Angel has given you a keyword *and* the necessary size of the square, then you may need to spend some time locating the proper Hebrew word to use and trying different spelling options to make it fit. Also, as you attempt to fit other words into the square, you may find it necessary to return to the keyword and try different ways of spelling it.

While you are doing this, also keep in mind that palindromes- words that are spelled the same when written forward or backward- are extremely desirable in the formulation of magickal word-squares. If you can find a keyword that fits your square and is naturally spelled the same when written forward and backward, then you will definitely want to use it.

On the other hand, there are some rare cases among Abraham's Talismans where a keyword is written forward and then backward to "force" a palindrome into the square. This seems to happen most often where the word is too small to fit into a larger square. For example, suppose your Guardian Angel has suggested a 7 x 7 square wherein the keyword is *Atah*- Hebrew for "Thou Art." Because *Atah* is only four letters long, you can lengthen it by transforming it into a seven—lettered palindrome:

A T A H A T A

Taking all of this together, the most perfect form a magickal word-square can take would be a Perfect Double Acrostic formed entirely of palindromes. This should always be your goal when compiling your own squares, though keep in mind it will not often be achievable.

Once you have your keyword, you will need to determine where in the square to place it. You have a couple of options here, depending on the size of the grid. In even-numbered squares, you will need to write the keyword around the circumference of the grid- this is what I call a "frame." For example, in the previously-illustrated Talisman for causing the Familiars to appear in the form of Eagles, the keyword N E S H E R was written as the frame of the square:

```
N E S H E R
E L E E H E
S E P P E H
H E P P E S
E H E E L E
R E H S E N
```

Of course, the above example is for a Perfect Double Acrostic. If your square were to become a regular Acrostic instead, you would only have a half-frame. For example, the Talisman I mentioned previously, to create visions in rings or jewellery, is an Acrostic with its keyword B E D S E R written in a half-frame:

```
B E D S E R
E L I E L A
D I A P I S
S E P P E S
E L I E M I
R A S S I N
```

On the other hand, if the grid is an odd-numbered size, you can either write the keyword in a frame, or it can be written in the very center, both across and downward. For instance, consider this Talisman from chapter 4, to create visions in the Moon:

```
C O H E N
O R A R E
H A S A H
E R A R O
N E H O C
```

Because this is the a 5x 5 grid, we find that one word- H A S A H- forms a central cross in the middle of the square. In Hebrew *Hazah* means "to sleep, dream"- which indicates the "visions" created by this Talisman are likely dreams during sleep. Also notice that H A S A H is a palindrome. If a square is going to be a

Perfect Double Acrostic, the central cross word *must* be a palindrome. If not, the square will have to be a regular Acrostic instead.

Where you choose to place the keyword of your square is a matter of trial-and-error, determined largely by the other words you find to add to the square. If you start with a frame but can't make it work, then (if the grid is odd-numbered) you can make it a central cross and try again.

Now that you understand some of the basics, we can continue with the rest of the process. It will take serious mental effort (not to mention use of the lexicon) to fill the rest of the square with letters.

I feel this is best illustrated with an example- therefore, let us suppose you wish to compile a square to find employment in a tough job market. I have consulted the Hebrew lexicon and found a good pool of words to work with. The best candidates for a keyword are:

Tamiid (TMYD) - "Continual employment"
Sekar (ShKR) - "To hire oneself out"

I also found these words, meaning "work", "workmen" or "labor":

Yetzer (YtzR)   *Etzeb* (AaTzB)   *Yalad* (YLD)
Maaseh (MAaShH) *Chashab* (ChShB) *Cabal* (KBL)
Charash (ChRSh) *Yagiya* (YGYAa)   *Amal* (AaML)
Malakah (MLAKH) *Abidah* (AaBIDH) *Paal* (PAaL)
Abad (AaBD)   *Aliliah* (AaLYLYH) *Paallah* (PAaLLH)
Abodah (AaBDH)   *Asah* (AaShH)

These are not all the words I could have listed. Plus, I could have searched for further related concepts such as "business", "wages", "position", etc, etc. I could have even resorted to checking Latin and Greek lexicons for even more options (though the best word-squares contain only one langage). You can generate a rather sizeable pool of words if you wish, but I think the above is good enough for our current illustration.

My primary choice for the keyword was *Tamid*- suggesting a 5 x 5 square. My first attempt was to write the keyword as a frame around the square, hoping to compile a Perfect Double Acrostic:

```
T A M I D
A       I
M       M
I       A
D I M A T
```

However, I quickly found that no suitable word in my pool (nor even when I re-checked the lexicon) began with an "A" and ended with an "I" (or "Y"). Nothing fit even when I attempted to be "creative" with the spellings! Thus this square was a dead end at the second line down. Therefore, I attempted the puzzle once more with the keyword in a half-frame, aiming for a regular Acrostic:

```
T A M I D            T A M I D
A                    A B O D A
M                    M O
I                    I D
D                    D A
```
Step 1   **Step 2**

As you can see, I was able to get a bit further this time. The word *Abodah* (AaBDH) was suitable for the second line with very little creativity in the transliteration. However, these puzzles become more difficult the further you go. Now that I have reached the third line down, I am forced to find a suitable word that begins with "Mo..." Sadly, I had no luck finding such a word, so this square is also a dead end.

Since this is an odd-numbered square, I had the final option of writing the keyword in the central cross. In this case a

Perfect Double Acrostic is ruled out (because *Tamid* is not a palindrome), but I could possibly score a regular Acrostic:

```
        T               Y E T Z R
        A               E Z A A B
T A M I D               T A M I D
        I               Z A I
        D               R B D
     Step 1              Step 2
```

In order to complete this square, I needed to find four words- one with a "T" in the center, one with an "A", another with an "I" and finally one with a central "D". With some creative transliteration, I was able to fit *Yetzer* into the first line, and *Etseb* into the second. Had this been a Perfect Double Acrostic, my work would have been complete, because the final two lines would have simply been the reverse of the first two. However, since I already ruled out that possibility, I was stuck trying to find two further words- one beginning with "Zai.." and another beginning with "Rbd..." That simply wasn't going to happen, so this square also turned out to be a dead end.

At this point, I decided to switch to my other favored keyword: *Sekar*. Again, this suggests a 5 x 5 square. And, once again, I will try to form a Perfect Double Acrostic by writing the keyword into the frame:

```
S A K A R        S A K A R        S A K A R
A       A        A B I D A        A B I D A
K       K        K I   I K        K I K I K
A       A        A D I B A        A D I B A
R A K A S        R A K A S        R A K A S
```
Step 1   **Step 2**   **Step 3**

This attempt was the pay-off. I only needed minor changes to the transliterations of both *Sekar* (ShKR) and *Abidah* (AaBIDH) in order to make them fit perfectly into the first two lines of the square. (Plus the changes I made are both acceptable transliterations of the Hebrew.) And, because this is a Perfect Double Acrostic, it was not necessary to find words for the final two lines.

Of course, you likely noticed that the "word" in the central cross doesn't appear to be a word at all. By the time I had filled in all the squares occupied by *Sekar* and *Abidah*, only the central cell of the entire grid was left open. By placing a "K" there, I formed a palindrome that completes this Perfect Double Acrostic. It may seem like a cheat, however Abraham appears to have used this technique on a large number of his own Talismans.

Using the above techniques, I was also able to compile a

second Perfect Double Acrostic square from my pool of words, using *Abad* (AaBD) and *Abodah* (AaBDH):

```
A A B A D
A B O D A
B O B O B
A D O B A
D A B A A
```

However, I consider this to be a square of lesser power. The words used for it both simply mean "work" - which is pretty vague when compared to the original two keywords I chose. However, the above A A B A D square should be perfectly useful for some matter related to work.

Working With Your Spirits

While the *Book of Abramelin* remains purposefully vague about the details of spirit conjuration, it has somewhat more to say about how to work with the spirits once you have conjured them. Some of this advice can be found in chapters seventeen and eighteen of Book II (Mathers' edition), just before the lists of spirit names. The rest is found in the final book, just after the chapters of Talismans.

Abraham stresses time and again that these spirits are of the chthonic type, and therefore certainly do pose a danger to the aspirant. It is true that his instruction is couched in typical Judeo-Christian rhetoric - such as the idea that these are fallen spirits, cast out from Heaven and sentenced to serve man. However, the advice he gives is not uncommon within even Pagan traditions that commonly deal with these types of spirits. For example, the Afrio-Caribbean faiths- such as *Santeria*, *Voudon* and *Palo-Mayombe*- offer similar warnings to their initiates, without the addition of Christian dogma. I will do much the same here.

As Abraham aptly points out, the spirits are not "little pet dogs." He also points out the spirits of this system are "of rank" - meaning they are not petty lesser spirits. They are powerful, and one must approach them with compassion and respect. Yet, at the same time, the Magus must simultaneously remain firmly in control- never letting his familiars forget who is in charge of the relationship. He is willing to reward them for a job well done, but not willing to give them treats merely because they demand them. And though he would (hopefully!) never mistreat his spirits, he always keeps in the fore of his mind how easily they could tear him to shreds if he is incompetent.

Also, the spirits you will gather to serve you will not necessarily *want* to do any work. For them, the best deal is to languish under your care- accepting your offerings and attention, while never being forced to earn their keep. Therefore, as Abraham warns us, the proud spirits will do everything in their power to get out of their oaths to you, and to eventually turn the tables so they are in control.

Of course, when it comes to spiritual entities, the danger is not merely physical. Remember the aspirant is supposed to receive from the sub-Princes those spirits who are most suited to his psychological make-up. Therefore, those same spirits are best suited to know and exploit your weaknesses. Abraham explains this rather well:

> "The spirits have so great knowledge that they comprehend very well by our actions what dispositions we have, and understand our inclinations, so that from the very beginning they prepare the way to make us to fail. If they know that a man is inclined unto vanity and pride,

they will humiliate themselves before him, and push that humility unto excess, and even unto idolatry, and this man will glory herein and become intoxicated with conceit, and the matter will not end without his commanding them some pernicious thing of such a nature that ultimately thence from will be derived that sin which will make the man the slave of the demon. Another man will be easily accessible to avarice, and then if he take not heed the malignant spirits will propose unto him thousands of ways of accumulating wealth, and of rendering himself rich by indirect and unjust ways and means, whence total restitution is afterwards difficult and even impossible, so that he who is in such case findeth himself ever the slave of the spirits. Another will be a man of letters; the spirits will inspire him with presumption, and he will then believe himself to be wiser even than the Prophets, furthermore they will endeavour to lead him astray in subtle points in matters appertaining unto God, and will make (that man) fall into a thousand errors, the which afterwards when he wisheth to support he will very frequently deny God, and his high mysteries. The causes and matters whereof (the spirits) will make use to cause a man to waver are infinite, especially when the man attempteth to make them submit to his commands, and this is why it is most necessary to be upon one's guard and to distrust oneself." [*The Book of the Sacred Magic of Abramelin the Mage*, Book III, "Essential remarks upon the foregoing symbols"]

As I have often heard from teachers of *Santeria* and *Palo*, you must never allow your spirits to "eat your head." That is to say, you must never allow them to get into your mind and turn the tables on you, because they will take any given opportunity to make you their slave. This is why Abraham warns us to command our spirits never to speak or act unless instructed. Otherwise they will have ample opportunities to confuse you and cause you to fail, and thereby finally slip free of your control.

All of this is why the spirit-magick of *Abramelin* is so obscured in the text. Practitioners of the occult arts are often all-too willing to open the manual to the final book and use the Talismans in any old fashion they choose. However, as Abraham stresses, it is vitally important that one first established Knowledge of and Conversation with the Holy Guardian Angel, and to never employ a spirit who has not sworn a formal oath to serve you. As you are dealing with entities who would rather enjoy a free ride and avoid working for you, it is necessary to have the authority of your Guardian behind your commands.

On the other hand, Abraham puts just as much stress upon

treating the spirits with kindness. Certainly the Magus must remain aloof to the spirits and treat them as a master would a servant. Yet, if they are serving you in accordance to their oaths and being humble toward you, then you must respond by treating them with all due respect. Just like the lion-tamer, you must strike a balance between the fact that you are the master and the fact that they could, if they had the desire and opportunity, destroy you with little effort. You must work to build your relationship, and make your spirits your allies.

Should your spirits disobey you, Abraham tells us the proper procedure for dealing with them. First and foremost, you must make sure the error is not your own. All of the spirits you have gathered in your Register are not of the same office and do not possess the same skills. (If they did, then it would be unnecessary to employ any spirit beyond the four Familiars.) Therefore, if a spirit will not execute a command you have given it, you must be absolutely sure you haven't called the wrong entity.

For instance, a spirit who can reveal information about the future is not likely going to be able to open locks for you. Or one who can bring armed men to protect you will probably not be able to heal your wounds. As we discussed previously in this essay, knowing what a spirit's name means can be a big help in judging what the spirit can do. And don't forget that simply *asking the spirit* is always a good first step.

If you discover that none of your current spirits are up to a given task, then you can employ the techniques for obtaining new Talismans and ask for a new spirit to add to your Register. Make sure to follow the full procedure, up to conjuring the Princes of Hell and having the new spirit swear the oath just like all the others.

However, if you know that your spirit is fully capable of performing a given task, but still refuses to obey, then you can employ disciplinary measures. The first step is to conjure the subPrince(s) in charge of the spirit, and have them directly command the spirit to follow out your wishes. You are to remind them of the oaths they have taken to you, and of the chastisement that awaits them if they, too, disobey.

If this does not work, the next step is to invoke the agent of that chastisement- your Holy Guardian Angel. Of course, doing this depends on the Angel having agreed to your intended goals. If he has, then it is only necessary to ask him to bring the spirits into line. The Guardian Angel is your whip, and the oath the spirits have sworn unto you is the chair.

I will now bring this essay to a close, though this certainly does not exhaust the subject of *Abramelin*'s magickal system. I have focused strictly upon the somewhat hidden system of spirit magick dispersed throughout the manuscript, as well as explained (perhaps for the first time) the method of constructing proper word-square Talismans. In order to save space, I have passed over most of Abraham's advice concerning the spirits during the three days of the Convocation- such as how to write the conjurations and how to address the Princes when they arrive, etc. However, most of the same concepts can be found described at length in chapter twelve of my *Secrets of the Magickal Grimoires*. I will certainly release more of my researches into and experiences with the *Abramelin* system in the future. Plus, you can check the bibliography of this essay for links to further resources.

May your spirits be prompt and trustworthy in all things!

Bibliography and Resources

AGRIPPA, H.C., April 11, 2004-last update, *Heinrich Cornelius Agrippa: Of Occult Philosophy, Book II. (part 1)* [Homepage of Twilit Grotto: Archives of Western Esoterica], [Online]. Available:
http://www.esotericarchives.com/agrippa/agrippa2.htm.

BARRETT, FRANCIS, 1801, *The Magus*, [ONLINE] Available http://www.sacred-texts.com/grim/magus/

CROSSWALK.COM, *The Old Testament Hebrew Lexicon*, [ONLINE] Available
http://www.biblestudytools.com/Lexicons/OldTestamentHebrew/
The New Testament Greek Lexicon, [ONLINE] Available

http://www.biblestudytools.com/Lexicons/NewTestamentGreek/

DEHN, GEORG, September 2006, *The Book of Abramelin: A New Translation*, Nicolas Hays, Inc.

FISHER, DAVE, Word Squares: Forerunners to Crossword Puzzles, [ONLINE] Avaialable
http://puzzles.about.com/library/weekly/aa030528.htm

HEIDRICK, BILL, 1987, An Abramelin Ramble, With Visits to Roadside Attractions Along the Way and Sundry Personal Advice, [ONLONE] Available
http://www.digital-brilliance.com/kab/abramel.htm

LEITCH, AARON, 2007, *Abramelin's Magical Word Squares: Compiled and Corrected for the First Time*, [ONLINE] Available:
http://kheph777.tripod.com/abrasquares.pdf

    2005. *Secrets of the Magickal Grimoires*. Woodbury, MN: Llewellyn Publications.

    2004, The Holy Guardian Angel: Exploring the Sacred Magick of Abramelin the Mage,
    [ONLINE] Available:
http://kheph777.tripod.com/art_HGA.html

PETERSON, JOSEPH (ed.), 1999, *Lemegeton Clavicula Solomonis or The Lesser Key of Solomon*,
[ONLINE] Available
http://www.esotericarchives.com/solomon/lemegeton.htm

MATHERS, SAMUEL, 1974, *The Book of the Sacred Magic of Abramelin the Mage*, Dover Publications. [Also at the Homepage of Twilit Grotto: Archives of Western Esoterica], [Online].

Available:

http://www.esotericarchives.com/abramelin/abramelin.htm

PERSEUS PROJECT, *Online Latin Lexicon*, [ONLINE]
Available:

http://www.perseus.tufts.edu/cgi-bin/resolveform?lang=Latin

Notes

1 In the French/Mathers version. Compare to *The Magus*, Book II, "Of the making of the Crystal and the form of preparation for a Vision."

2 In the German version. Compare to the wax Almadel of Solomon described in the *Lemegeton*, as well as to John Dee's wax Seal of Truth described in his Enochian journals- both of which are intended to facilitate angelic visions.

3 Leviathan is associated directly with Satan, or Satan's power, mainly in Christian mythos. See
http://en.wikipedia.org/wiki/Leviathan

4 Mathers did some work toward offering loose "translations" for many of the spirits names in his edition of the Book of Abramelin. I hope to provide updated notations based on Dehn's edition soon.

Abramelin's Magickal Word Squares
Compiled and Corrected for the First Time

The following word-squares (or "acrostics") have been complied from Book IV of George Dehn and Steven Guth's English translation of the *Book of Abramelin*. These are the completed squares taken from the German original(s), rather than the corrupted and incomplete versions found in the French recension translated by S. L. Mathers.

However, in this new translation, Mr. Dehn did not compile the magickal words into grid-squares. (According to his notes, the manuscripts he used for his translation contained the words written only in line form.) Therefore, I have undertaken the task of inserting them into proper grids. What follows is the first time English speaking students have seen the Abramelin word squares in their compiled (and corrected) form.

As I placed Abramelin's words into their grids, I discovered a large number of errors. (Most of them apparently from the original manuscript, and not the fault of Mr. Dehn or Mr. Guth!) Some were apparent transcription errors- such as confounding "c" and "e", "f" and "s", or "b" and "k". I also found several places where adjacent letters were transposed- similar to writing the word "receive" as "recieve." Some of the errors seemed unexplainable, unless they were deliberate blinds. Lending weight to that theory, I also found a few of the squares inverted, backward or mis-labeled.

In each case of correction, I have also included Dehn's text of the original square in a footnote. Out of 242 squares, I have found approximately 156 in need of correction- not counting several instances where labels were applied to the wrong squares. Only one square in the entire set was irreparable.

Methods of Correction

The easiest squares to correct were the simple Acrostics and the 'Perfect' Double Acrostics- both of which contain repeated patterns throughout the square. It was more difficult to judge the regular Double Acrostics, though I have made my best attempts to correct them where necessary. There were very few cases where I had to choose between one letter or another, or even fill in a missing letter. In such cases I would either go with intuition (usually based on the overall pattern in the square), and/or analyze the square linguistically to discover an acceptable spelling. (The latter was often used to confirm or correct the former.)

I also compared Dehn's work to the French recension each step along the way. Mathers' notes have been surprisingly useful (given the sorry state of the text he was using)- and I have referenced each case where his notations aided me in correcting a square.

As a side note: I suspect the author of the French version was working on these same corrections, but left the task incomplete. With this document, the French author's long-awaited goal is finally realized.

Further Analysis Ongoing...

This document is only a presentation of the corrected Abramelin squares, with notes explaining the differences between my squares and Mr. Dehn's. I have not included the bulk of my linguistic analysis of the words themselves, as that work is ongoing. I have already compared the Abramelin squares to *all* of Mathers' linguistic notes, and cross-referenced both to Biblical Hebrew, Greek and Latin Lexicons. I am, of course, also using the Lexicons to find etymologies that Mathers missed (most often due to the corruption of the French squares).

In many cases, the linguistic "decoding" of a square has resulted in further corrections to its lettering. I have nearly completed the Hebrew analysis (save for a few squares that have eluded me, and may not turn out to be Hebrew at all), and some of the Greek and Latin as well. Fortunately, the Abramelin squares are overwhelmingly based upon Hebrew, so I do not expect any further significant corrections to the squares' lettering. In the case

of further corrections, I will update this manuscript in the future.
My complete linguistic analysis will appear in a later work.

    Aaron Leitch
    March 2007

Chapter 1: To Discover Past and Future Things, but Not Against the Will of God.

1/1. To Know Things Past

M	O	R	E	H
O	R	I	R	E
R	I	N	I	R
E	R	I	R	O
H	E	R	O	M

1/2. Future Things

N	A	B	H	I
A	D	A	I	H
B	A	R	A	B
H	I	A	D	A
I	H	B	A	N

1/3. Future Things

T	H	I	R	A	M	A
H	I	G	A	N	A	M
I	G	O	G	A	N	A
R	A	G	I	G	A	R
A	N	A	G	O	G	I
M	A	N	A	G	I	H
A	M	A	R	I	H	T

1/4. To Know Future Things in War

M	I	L	O	N
I	R	A	G	O
L	A	M	A	L
O	G	A	R	I
N	O	L	I	M

1/5. Past and Forgotten Things

M	A	L	A	C	H
A	M	A	N	E	C
L	A	N	A	N	A
A	N	A	N	A	L
C	E	N	A	M	A
H	C	A	L	A	M

1/6. To Foretell Coming Sorrows

N	U	D	E	T	O	N
U	S	I	L	A	R	O
D	I	R	E	M	A	T
E	L	E	M	E	L	E
T	A	M	E	R	I	D
O	R	A	L	I	S	U
N	O	T	E	D	U	N

1/7. Future Things

M	E	L	A	M	M	E	D
E	R	I	F	O	I	S	E
L	I	S	I	L	L	I	M
A	F	I	R	E	L	O	M
M	O	L	E	R	I	F	A
M	I	L	L	I	S	I	L
E	S	I	O	F	I	R	E
D	E	M	M	A	L	E	M

1/8. Past things[1]

E	K	D	I	L	U	N
K	L	I	S	A	T	U
D	I	N	A	N	A	L
I	S	A	G	A	S	I
L	A	N	A	N	I	D
U	T	A	S	I	L	K
N	U	L	I	D	K	E

1/9. To Foretell Frosts and Miracles

S	A	R	A	P	I
A	R	A	I	R	P
R	A	K	K	I	A
A	I	K	K	A	R
P	R	I	A	R	A
I	P	A	R	A	S

---

1 Dehn: EKDILON, KLISATU, DINANAL, ISAGASI, LANANID, UTASILK, NULIDKE

1/10. Future Things[2]

K	O	S	E	M
O	B	O	D	E
S	O	F	O	S
E	D	O	B	O
M	E	S	O	K

Note on 1/10: Mathers' note on this square was helpful. Qasam (QSM) means "to divine, diviner" in OT Hebrew.

1/11. Future Things

A	L	L	U	P
L	E	I	R	U
L	I	G	I	L
U	R	I	E	L
P	U	L	L	A

---

2 Dehn: LOSEM, OBODE, SOFOS, EDOBO, MESOL

Chapter 2: To Have Reports on Doubtful Things

2/1.[3]

P	O	T	H	E	R
O	T	H	A	R	E
T	H	O	R	A	H
H	A	R	O	H	T
E	R	A	H	T	O
R	E	H	T	O	P

2/2.

M	E	L	A	B	B	E	D
E	L	I	N	A	L	S	E
L	I	K	A	K	I	L	B
A	N	A	K	A	K	A	B
B	A	K	A	K	A	N	A
B	L	I	K	A	K	I	L
E	S	L	A	N	I	L	E
D	E	B	B	A	L	E	M

---

3   Dehn: POTHER, OTHARE, THORAH, HAROHT, ERAHTO, REHTOP

2/3.

M	E	B	H	A	E	R
E	L	I	A	I	L	E
B	I	K	O	S	I	A
H	A	O	R	O	A	H
A	I	S	O	K	I	B
E	L	I	A	I	L	E
R	E	A	H	B	E	M

Chapter 3: To Make Every Spirit Appear

3/1. In the Shape of a Dragon

M	A	R	L	I	F	I	M
I	T	H	I	S	I	R	O
D	S	E	K	E	N	I	M
A	T	R	A	R	A	T	U
T	I	R	A	R	A	I	N
M	I	N	E	K	E	S	D
O	L	A	R	A	H	L	A
S	O	M	F	I	R	O	S

3/2. In Human Shape

S	A	T	A	N
A	D	A	M	A
T	A	B	A	T
A	M	A	D	A
N	A	T	A	S

3/3. In Animal Shape

L	I	R	B	I	A	C
E	S	A	E	R	M	I
R	A	S	H	E	U	P
F	I	L	E	M	I	R
I	S	A	M	A	N	O
R	E	R	O	L	I	N
I	R	E	T	I	S	U

3/4. In Bird Shape[4]

B	E	M	T	A	M	A
E	M	A	S	D	A	R
M	A	K	I	U	R	O
T	S	I	P	P	O	R
A	D	U	P	O	S	E
M	A	R	O	S	A	L
A	R	O	R	E	L	I

Note on 3/4: The above is my best attempt at correcting this square.

---

4   Dehn: BEMTAUL, EMASDAI, MAKIURO, ESIPPOS, ADAPOSA, MAROMAD, ARORELI

Chapter 4: To Create Visions

4/1. In Mirrors, Glass and Crystals[5]

G	I	L	I	O	N	I	M
I	R	I	M	I	I	R	I
L	I	O	S	A	S	I	N
I	M	S	A	R	A	I	O
O	I	A	R	A	S	M	I
N	I	S	A	S	O	I	L
I	R	I	I	M	I	R	I
M	I	N	O	I	L	I	G

4/2. In Caves, Vaults, Crypts and Grottos Underground

E	T	H	A	N	I	M
T	I	A	D	I	S	I
H	A	R	A	P	I	N
A	D	A	M	A	D	A
N	I	P	A	R	A	H
I	S	I	D	A	I	T
M	I	N	A	H	T	E

---

5   Dehn: GILIONIM, IRIMIRI, LIOSASIN, IMSARAIO, OIARASMI, NITASOIL, IRIIMITI, MINOILIG

4/3. In the Air

A	P	P	A	R	E	T
P	A	R	E	S	T	E
P	R	E	R	E	O	R
A	E	R	E	R	E	A
R	O	E	R	E	R	P
E	T	S	E	R	A	P
T	E	R	A	P	P	A

4/4. In Jewels and Rings[6]

B	E	D	S	E	R
E	L	I	E	L	A
D	I	A	P	I	S
S	E	P	P	E	S
E	L	I	E	M	I
R	A	S	S	I	N

Note on 4/4: Mathers' note was helpful.

Betser (BtzR) indicates gold or a golden ring.

4/5. In Beeswax and Through Writing[7]

L	O	C	E	N
O	T	A	R	A
C	A	R	A	G
E	R	A	M	I
N	A	G	I	D

Note on 4/5: This square appeared to be backward in the German text.

---

6   Dehn: BEDSEK, ELIELA, DIAPIS, SEPPES, ELIEMI, KATSIN
7   Dehn: NECOL, ARATO, GARAC, IMARE, DIGAN

4/6. Through Fire

N	A	S	I
A	P	I	S
S	I	P	A
I	S	A	N

4/7. In the Moon

C	O	H	E	N
O	R	A	R	E
H	A	S	A	H
E	R	A	R	O
N	E	H	O	C

4/8. In Water

A	D	M	O	N
D	R	A	S	O
M	A	I	A	M
O	S	A	R	D
N	O	M	D	A

4/9. In the Hand[8]

H	E	L	E	L
E	D	A	G	E
L	A	D	A	L
E	G	A	D	E
L	E	L	E	H

Note on 4/9: This square appeared to be upside-down in the German text.

---

8   Dehn: LELEH, EGADE, LADAL, EDAGE, HELEL

Chapter 5: To obtain Familiar Spirits, Bound or Free, and to Send Them Away

5/1. In the Form of a Giant

A	N	A	K	I	M
N	I	L	A	R	I
A	L	I	S	A	K
K	A	S	I	L	A
I	R	A	L	I	N
M	I	K	A	N	A

5/2. As a Page[9]

O	I	K	E	T	I	S
I	P	O	R	A	S	I
K	E	L	I	R	A	T
E	N	I	P	I	N	E
T	A	R	I	A	R	K
I	D	E	N	S	A	I
S	I	T	E	K	I	O

Note on 5/2: This square has a Frame and palindrome Cross, and appears to *want* to be an Acrostic or 'Perfect' Double Acrostic. However, my best attempt to correct it results only in a Double Acrostic. (Mathers' note was helpful. Oiketis is Greek for "slaves" or "head wife.")

---

9 Dehn: OIKETIS, IPORASI, KELIRAL, ENIPINE, LARIARK, IDENSAI, SILEKIO

5/3. As a Soldier[10]

P	A	R	A	S
A	H	A	R	A
R	A	C	A	R
A	R	A	H	A
S	A	R	A	P

5/4. In the Form of a Flower[11]

P	E	R	A	C	H	I
E	R	I	P	E	I	H
R	I	M	E	N	E	C
A	P	E	R	E	P	A
C	E	N	E	M	I	R
H	I	E	P	I	R	E
I	H	C	A	R	E	P

5/5. As an Old Man[12]

R	I	Z	I	R
I	S	A	R	I
Z	A	K	E	N
I	R	E	P	I
R	I	N	I	R

Note on 5/5: Zaken (ZQN) is Hebrew for "old man."

---

10 Dehn: PARAS, AHARA, RACAR, ARASA, SARAP
11 Dehn: PERACHI, ERIPEIH, RIMENEC, APEREPA, CENEMIR, HIEPIRE, IHVAREP
12 Dehn: RITIR, ISARI, RAKEN, IREPI, RITIR

5/6. As a Rider

R	A	C	A	B
A	R	I	P	A
C	I	L	I	C
A	P	I	R	A
B	A	C	A	R

5/7. As a Negro in Appearance[13]

C	U	S	I	S
U	E	A	H	I
S	A	R	A	S
I	H	A	E	U
S	I	S	U	C

5/8. As an Eagle[14]

N	E	S	H	E	R
E	L	E	E	H	E
S	E	P	P	E	H
H	E	P	P	E	S
E	H	E	E	L	E
R	E	H	S	E	N

---

13 Dehn: CUSIS, VEAHI, SARAS, IHAEN, SISUC
14 Dehn: NESHER, ELEEHE, HEPPEH, SEPPES, EHEELE, REHSEN

5/9. As a Snake

P	E	T	H	E	N
E	R	A	A	N	E
T	A	R	C	A	H
H	A	C	R	A	T
E	N	A	A	R	E
N	E	H	T	E	P

5/10. As a Lion[15]

K	E	F	E	R
E	R	A	R	E
F	A	M	A	F
E	R	A	R	E
R	E	F	E	K

Note on 5/10: Kephyr (KPhYR) is Hebrew for "young lion."

5/11. As a Dog[16]

K	O	B	H	A
O	R	A	I	H
B	A	L	A	B
H	I	A	R	O
A	H	B	O	K

---

15 Dehn: KELEF, ERARE, LAMAL, ERARE, KELEF
16 Dehn: KOBHA, ORAIH, BALAH, HIARO, AHBEK

5/12. As a Monkey[17]

C	E	P	H	I	R
E	L	A	D	I	I
P	A	R	I	E	H
H	E	I	R	A	P
I	I	D	A	L	E
R	I	H	P	E	C

Note on 5/12: This square was badly damaged. Given the evidence, it appears a perfect double acrostic was intended. Therefore I based my reconstruction upon that assumption.

---

17 Dehn: CEPHIR, ELADI, PARIEH, HEIROP, HIALE, RIPHAE

Chapter Six: For Working Mines

6/1. To do Everything so that Shafts do not Collapse in Mines[18]

S	E	L	A	A	H
E	R	A	N	D	A
L	A	M	A	N	A
A	N	A	M	A	L
A	D	N	A	R	E
H	A	A	L	E	S

Note on 6/1: Selah means "to lift up, exalt" in OT Hebrew.

6/2. To Show the Location of Gold or Silver Veins[19]

A	L	E	A	B	R	U	H	I
L	I	R	M	U	A	P	I	H
E	R	A	I	B	R	I	P	U
A	M	I	D	A	M	R	A	R
B	U	B	A	U	A	B	U	B
R	A	R	M	A	D	I	M	A
U	P	I	R	B	I	A	R	E
H	I	P	A	U	M	R	I	L
I	H	U	R	B	A	E	L	A

---

18 Dehn: FELAAH, ERANDA, LAMANA, ANAMAL, HALEF
19 Dehn: ALEABRUHI, LIRMUAPI, ERAIBRIPU, ANIDAMRAR, BUBAUABUB, RARMADINA, UPIRBIARE, HIPAUMRIL, IHURBAELA

6/3. To do all Sorts of Mining Work

K	I	L	O	I	N
I	S	E	R	P	I
L	E	N	I	R	O
O	R	I	N	E	L
I	P	R	E	S	I
N	I	O	L	I	K

6/4. To do Mining with Tunnels

N	A	K	A	B
A	N	I	N	A
K	I	R	I	K
A	N	I	N	A
B	A	K	A	N

6/5. To Take Water Out of Mines and Shafts[20]

P	E	L	A	G	I	N
E	R	E	L	O	L	I
L	E	R	E	P	O	G
A	L	E	M	E	L	A
G	O	P	E	R	E	L
I	L	O	L	E	R	E
N	I	G	A	L	E	P

---

20 Dehn: PELAGIN, ERENOLI, LEREPOG, ALEMELA, GOPEREL, ILONERE, NIGALEP

6/6. For the Spirits to Bring Wood for Smelting[21]

K	I	T	T	I	K
I	S	I	A	D	I
T	I	N	N	A	T
T	A	N	N	I	T
I	D	A	I	S	I
K	I	T	T	I	K

Note on 6/6: This square was corrected in Mathers' edition of the French text.

---

21 Dehn: KITTIP, IFIADI, TANNAL, FINIT, IDRASI, KITTIK

6/7. To Purify the Ore

M	A	R	A	K
A	L	A	P	A
R	A	N	A	R
A	P	A	L	A
K	A	R	A	M

6/8. To do Various Mining Works

G	A	D	R	A	R
A	I	R	A	P	A
D	R	A	M	A	R
R	A	M	A	R	D
A	P	A	R	I	A
R	A	R	D	A	G

Chapter Seven:
To Have the Spirits Perform Alchemical Work

7/1. To Have the Spirits Bring Forth All Sorts of Metals Through Chemical Work[22]

M	E	T	A	L	O
E	Z	A	T	E	L
T	A	R	A	T	A
A	T	A	R	A	T
L	E	T	A	Z	E
O	L	A	T	E	M

7/2. To Have the Spirits Do All Sorts of Chemical Work[23]

T	A	B	B	A	T
A	R	U	N	C	A
B	U	I	R	N	B
B	N	R	I	U	B
A	C	N	U	R	A
T	A	B	B	A	T

---

22 Dehn: METALO, EZATEH, TARATA, ATARAT, HETAZE, OLATEM
23 Dehn: TABBAT, ARUNCA, BUIRUB, BURIUB, ACNURA, TABBAT

7/3. To Learn All Sorts of Alchemical Arts From the Spirits[24]

I	P	O	M	A	N	O
P	A	M	E	R	A	M
O	M	A	L	O	N	I
M	E	L	A	C	A	H
A	R	O	C	A	M	I
N	A	N	A	M	O	N
O	M	I	H	I	N	I

---

24 Dehn: IPOMANO, PAMERAM, ONALOMI, MELACAH, ARORAMI, NANAMON, OMIHINI

Chapter Eight: To Make or Prevent Storms

8/1. To Make Hail[25]

C	A	N	A	M	A	L
A	M	A	D	A	M	A
N	A	D	A	H	A	M
A	D	A	M	A	D	A
M	A	H	A	D	A	N
A	M	A	D	A	M	A
L	A	M	A	N	A	C

8/2. To Make a Heavy, Short Shower[26]

S	A	G	R	I	R
A	S	I	A	N	I
G	I	R	I	A	R
R	A	I	R	I	G
I	N	A	I	S	A
R	I	R	G	A	S

---

25 Dehn: CANAMAL, AMADAME, NADAHAM, ADAMAHA, MEHADAM, AMAHANA, LOMANAC
26 Dehn: SAGRIR, AFIANI, HIRIAS, RAIRIG, MAISA, RIRGAS

8/3. To Make Snow and Ice

T	A	K	A	T
A	T	E	T	A
K	E	R	E	K
A	T	E	T	A
T	A	K	A	T

8/4. To Make a Thunderstorm

H	A	M	A	H
A	B	A	L	A
M	A	H	A	M
A	L	A	B	A
H	A	M	A	H

Chapter Nine: To Transform People into Animals and Animals into People

9/1. People into Donkeys[27]

I	E	M	I	M	E	I
E	R	I	O	N	T	E
M	I	R	T	I	E	M
I	O	T	I	T	A	I
M	N	I	T	I	U	M
E	T	E	A	U	R	E
I	E	M	I	M	E	I

9/2. People into Deer[28]

A	I	A	C	I	L	A
I	S	I	O	R	E	L
A	I	C	R	I	R	I
C	O	R	I	R	O	C
I	R	I	R	C	I	A
L	E	R	O	I	S	I
A	L	I	C	A	I	A

Note on 9/2: The above is my best attempt to correct this square.

---

27 Dehn: JEMIMEJ, ERIONTE, MIRTIEM, FOTIFAI, MINTIUM, ETEAURE, JEMIMEJ
28 Dehn: AIACILA, ISIOREL, AICRIRA, CORILON, IRILCIA, LERUIST, ALINAIA

9/3. Animals into People[29]

I	S	I	C	H	A	D	A	M	I	O	N
S	E	R	R	A	R	E	P	I	N	T	O
I	R	A	A	S	I	M	E	L	E	I	S
C	R	A	T	I	B	A	R	I	N	S	T
H	A	S	I	N	A	S	U	O	T	I	R
A	R	I	B	A	T	I	N	T	I	R	A
D	E	M	A	S	I	C	O	A	N	O	S
A	P	E	R	U	N	O	I	L	E	M	I
M	I	L	I	O	T	A	L	U	L	E	L
I	N	E	N	T	I	N	E	L	I	T	A
O	T	I	S	I	R	O	M	E	T	I	S
N	O	S	T	R	A	S	I	L	A	S	I

Note on 9/3: This square was badly damaged, and I've done my best to correct it. The French author made a similar attempt to correct the square, which you can see in Mathers' edition.

---

29 Dehn: ISICHADAMION, SERRAREPINTO, IRAASIMELEIS, ORATIBARINP, HARINSTUOTIR, ARABATINTIRA, DEMASICOANOS, APERUNOILEMI, MILIOTABUEL, NIONTINOLITA, OTISIRIMELIS, NOSTRACILARI

9/4. People into Wild Pigs[30]

C	H	A	D	S	I	R
H	A	R	I	A	N	I
A	R	O	R	I	A	S
D	I	R	A	R	I	D
S	A	I	R	O	R	A
I	N	A	I	R	A	H
R	I	S	D	A	H	C

Note on 9/4: Mathers' note on the word CHADSIR was helpful with this square. The word ChZYR (Mathers has "ChZR") means "wild boar" in Old Testament Hebrew.

9/5. People into Dogs[31]

E	L	E	T	R	A	K
L	I	R	E	E	P	E
E	R	O	M	A	I	L
T	E	M	U	M	E	T
R	E	A	M	O	R	E
A	P	I	E	R	I	P
K	E	L	T	E	P	H

Note on 9/5: This square appeared to be upside down in the German text.

---

30 Dehn: CHADRIS, HARIANI, ARORIAS, DIRALID, SOALIRA, MAIRAH, RISDAHE
31 Dehn: KEKEPH, APIERIP, RELMORE, REMUNAT, ERONAIL, TIRAILE, ELETRAK

9/6. People into Wolves[32]

D	I	S	E	E	B	E	H
I	S	A	R	T	R	I	E
S	A	R	H	O	A	S	B
E	R	H	E	T	R	O	E
E	T	O	T	M	A	T	E
B	R	A	R	A	R	I	S
E	I	S	O	T	I	T	I
H	E	B	E	E	S	I	D

Note on 9/6: This was an extremely difficult square. The above is my best attempt at correction, working from the assumption that a regular Acrostic was intended. (The French version attempts to repair it, but assumes it is a Double Acrostic. See Mathers' translation.)

9/7. Animals into Stone[33]

B	E	D	A	S	E	K
E	F	I	R	A	M	E
D	I	R	M	I	A	S
A	R	M	F	I	I	A
S	A	I	I	A	R	D
E	M	A	I	R	T	E
K	E	S	A	D	E	B

---

32 Dehn: DISCEBEH, ISARTRIC, SARHIAB, ERBETRE, ETOMMATE, BARIURIS, ERSONITI, HEMANAD

33 Dehn: BEDASEK, EFIRAME, DIRMIAS, AMAFIA, SAIIARD, EMAIRTE, KERADEB

Chapter Ten: To Prevent and Remove All Other Magick

10/1. To Heal Magickal Sicknesses[34]

C	O	L	I
O	D	A	L
L	A	C	A
I	L	A	R

10/2. To Prevent Magickal Storms[35]

S	E	A	R	A	H
E	L	L	O	P	A
A	L	A	T	I	M
R	O	T	A	R	A
A	P	I	R	A	C
H	A	M	A	C	S

Note on 10/2: Sa'arah is OT Hebrew for "storm."

---

34 Dehn: COLI, ODAL, LOCA, IEAR
35 Dehn: SEARAS, ELLOPA, ALATIM, ROTARA, APIRAC, HAMAIS

10/3. When a Magician is in the Air Making a Cloud, so That he Falls to Earth[36]

N	E	I	S	I	E	N
E	R	E	A	E	R	E
I	E	R	P	R	E	I
S	A	P	I	P	A	S
I	E	R	P	R	E	I
E	R	E	A	E	R	E
N	E	I	S	I	E	N

10/4. Expose Hidden Appearances

H	O	R	A	H
O	S	O	M	A
R	O	T	O	R
A	M	O	S	O
H	A	R	O	H

---

36 Dehn: NEISIEN, EREAERE, IREPREI, SAPIPAS, IERPERI, EREAERE, NEISIEN

10/5. Expose Hidden Magicians[37]

P	A	R	A	D	I	L	O	N
A	R	I	N	O	C	I	S	O
R	I	L	A	R	L	A	I	L
A	N	A	T	A	L	L	C	I
D	O	R	A	T	A	R	O	D
I	C	L	L	A	T	N	A	
L	I	A	L	R	A	L	I	R
O	S	I	C	O	N	I	R	A
N	O	L	I	D	A	R	A	P

Note on 10/5: This square was very confusing. It appears to be intended as a 'Perfect' Double Acrostic. The above is my best attempt at correction.

---

37 Dehn: PARACLILIU, ARINOCISO, RILARLAIL, ANOTALECU, DORATACAL, ICALAFANA, LIELCARIT, OSICONIRA, NOCILATAM

10/6. To Make a Magician's Soldiers Disappear[38]

L	U	D	A	C	A	M
U	N	E	L	I	R	A
D	E	R	A	R	O	C
A	L	A	H	A	L	A
C	I	R	A	C	U	N
A	R	O	L	U	S	E
M	A	C	A	N	E	S

Note on 10/6: After correction, this square appeared to be upside down. (I'm not entirely certain.) The French author made a similar attempt at correction, but without flipping it. See Mathers.

10/7. Hold This Square in Your Hand to Prevent Magick From Working[39]

I	K	K	E	B	E	K	K	I
K	A	R	T	U	T	R	A	K
K	R	U	T	U	T	U	R	K
E	T	T	S	A	S	T	T	E
B	U	U	A	R	A	U	U	B
E	T	T	S	A	S	T	T	E
K	R	U	T	U	T	U	R	K
K	A	R	T	U	T	R	A	K
I	K	K	E	B	E	K	K	I

---

38 Dehn: MACANES, AROLUSE, CIRACUN, ALAHALA, DERARPE, UNETIRA, LUDASAM
39 Dehn: IKKEBEKKI, KARTUTRAK, KRUTUTURK, ETISATISE, BUTARATUB, ESITASITE, KRUTUTURK, KARTUTRAK, IKKEBEKKI

Chapter Eleven:
To Obtain Lost Books, Hidden Manuscripts, Etc.

11/1. Astronomical Books[40]

M	I	B	A	H	O	C
I	N	O	R	A	R	O
B	O	R	E	R	I	D
A	R	E	H	P	E	S
H	A	R	P	I	N	E
O	R	I	E	N	T	I
C	O	D	S	E	I	M

Note on 11/1: Once corrected, this square appeared to be upside down.

11/2. Magickal Books

L	A	C	H	A	L
A	R	A	I	B	A
C	A	L	A	I	H
H	I	A	L	A	C
A	B	I	A	R	A
L	A	H	C	A	L

---

40 Dehn: CODSEIM, ORIENTI, HARPINE, AREHPES, BORDERID, INONARO, MIBAHRE

11/3. Pharmacopeia[41]

K	E	H	A	H	E	K
E	N	I	F	I	N	E
H	I	R	I	R	I	H
A	F	I	R	I	F	A
H	I	R	I	R	I	H
E	N	I	F	I	N	E
K	E	H	A	H	E	K

---

41 Dehn: KEHAHEK, ENIFINE, HIRIRIH, AFIRISA, HIRIRIH, ENIFINE, KEHAHEK

Chapter Twelve: To Discover the Hidden Plans and Plots of a Person

12/1. Secrets From Letters or Talk[42]

M	E	G	I	L	L	A
E	P	R	E	I	A	L
G	R	U	N	T	A	L
I	E	N	I	U	R	I
L	I	T	U	R	O	G
L	A	A	R	O	N	E
A	L	L	I	G	E	M

12/2. Secrets From Words

S	I	M	B	A	S	I
I	R	U	A	R	I	S
M	U	R	K	A	R	A
B	A	K	A	K	A	B
A	R	A	K	R	U	M
S	I	R	A	U	R	I
I	S	A	B	M	I	S

---

42 Dehn: MEGILLA, EPREIAL, HURUNTAL, IENIURS, LITUROG, CAARONO, ALIGEM

12/3. Hidden Works of a Person[43]

M	A	A	B	H	A	D
A	D	S	A	I	S	A
A	S	A	D	R	I	H
B	A	D	A	D	A	B
H	I	R	D	A	S	A
A	S	I	A	S	D	A
D	A	H	B	A	A	M

12/4. Secret War Plans[44]

M	I	L	C	H	A	M	A	H
I	R	O	H	I	D	E	N	A
L	O	P	A	L	I	D	E	M
C	H	A	K	A	R	I	D	A
H	I	L	A	H	A	L	I	H
A	D	I	R	A	K	A	H	C
M	E	D	I	L	A	P	O	L
A	N	E	D	I	H	O	R	I
H	A	M	A	H	C	L	I	M

Note on 12/4: Mathers' note was helpful with this square. Milchamah (MLChMH) is OT Hebrew for "war, warriors."

---

43 Dehn: MAABHAD, ADSAISA, ARADRIH, BADAKAB, HIRKORA, ASCADSA, DACHBAM
44 Dehn: MILEHAMAH, IROHIDEIRA, LOPALIDEM, CHAKARIDA, HILAHALIK, ADIRACHHE, MEDILAPOL, ANEDIHORI, HAMAHCLIM

12/5. To Discover Sexual Activity[45]

J	E	D	I	D	A	H
E	N	E	T	E	K	A
D	E	R	A	R	E	D
I	T	A	M	A	T	I
D	E	R	A	R	E	D
A	K	E	T	E	N	E
H	A	D	I	D	E	J

12/6. The Hidden Riches and Treasures of a Person

A	S	A	M	I	M
S	I	L	A	P	A
A	L	I	G	I	L
M	A	G	I	D	E
I	P	I	D	R	E
M	A	L	E	E	M

12/7. The Hidden Arts of a Person[46]

M	E	L	A	C	A	H
E	R	O	B	O	L	A
L	O	R	A	R	I	B
A	B	A	H	A	D	U
C	O	R	A	L	I	C
A	L	I	D	I	N	E
H	A	B	U	C	E	M

---

45 Dehn: JEDIDAH, ENITEKA, DERARED, ITAMUNI, DERARED, ALLTINE, HADIDEI

46 Dehn: MELACAH, EROBOLO, LORAFIL, ABAHADN, CORALIC, ALIDNE, HABUCEM

Chapter Thirteen:

To Make a Dead Person Walk for Seven Years

13/1. That he Does and Talks Like a Living Person From Sunrise to Noon[47]

R	E	L	B	E	L	A	C
E	R	A	R	I	I	N	I
L	A	L	I	N	A	A	K
B	R	I	L	F	R	P	I
E	I	N	F	I	N	A	K
L	I	A	R	N	B	S	I
A	N	A	P	A	S	U	H
C	I	K	I	K	I	H	I

---

47 Dehn: RELBELAC, ERARMINI, BALISAAK, BRILURPI, EINFINAK, LIAREBI, ANAPASUH, HIKIRIBI

13/2. From Noon to Sunset[48]

M	E	T	H	I	R	R	A	H
E	N	I	A	S	A	E	N	A
T	I	B	M	A	I	L	I	R
H	O	F	I	B	R	U	A	R
I	U	I	B	R	I	N	S	I
R	O	S	A	E	S	T	A	H
R	I	F	N	A	I	A	U	T
A	S	A	C	H	I	R	T	E
H	A	R	R	I	H	T	E	M

13/3. From Sunset to Midnight[49]

M	A	P	P	A	L	A	H
A	T	R	I	N	I	N	A
P	R	I	R	I	S	I	N
P	I	R	E	A	O	M	A
A	N	I	A	T	N	A	T
L	I	S	O	N	P	E	H
A	N	I	M	A	E	S	A
H	A	N	A	T	H	A	N

Note on 13/3: This was a difficult correction. The above is my best attempt.

---

48 Dehn: METHIRRAH, ENIASAENA, BIBMAILIR, HOFIBRUAR, TUIBRINSI, ROSAESTAH, RIFNAIAUF, ASACHIRTE, HARRITHEM
49 Dehn: MAPPALAH, ATHRININA, PRINDEIRA, PIREUSON, ANIATKA, LISONPIT, ANIMAESA, HANATHAN

13/4. From Midnight to Sunrise[50]

P	E	G	E	R
E	N	I	A	E
G	I	S	I	G
E	A	I	N	E
R	E	G	E	P

---

50 Dehn: PEGER, ENIAE, GISIG, EAITE, REGEP

Chapter Fourteen: For Invisibility

14/1. First Hour[51]

A	L	A	M	A	L	A
L	I	R	A	R	I	L
A	R	O	T	O	R	A
M	A	T	A	T	A	M
A	R	O	T	O	R	A
L	I	R	A	R	I	L
A	L	A	M	A	L	A

14/2. Second Hour[52]

T	S	A	P	H	A	H
S	I	R	O	I	N	A
A	R	N	T	R	I	H
P	O	T	A	T	O	P
H	I	R	T	N	R	A
A	N	I	O	R	I	S
H	A	H	P	A	S	T

Note on 14/2: The above is my best attempt to correct this square.

---

51 Dehn: ALAMATA, LISAFIL, AROLORA, MATATAM, ARATORA, LISAFIL, ALAMATA
52 Dehn: ARAPHALI, SIRONIA, ARNTRAH, BETANOP, HIRNERA, ANIORIS, HAHPAST

14/3. Third Hour[53]

C	A	S	A	H
A	P	O	D	A
S	O	M	I	S
A	D	I	N	A
H	A	S	A	C

14/4. Fourth Hour[54]

A	L	A	T	A	H
L	I	S	A	N	A
A	S	O	G	A	T
T	A	G	O	S	A
A	N	A	S	I	L
H	A	T	A	L	A

14/5. Fifth Hour[55]

K	O	D	E	R
O	R	U	S	E
D	U	L	I	D
E	S	I	N	O
R	E	D	O	K

---

53 Dehn: CASALI, APODA, SOMIS, ADINA, HASAC
54 Dehn: ALATAH, LISANA, AROGAT, TAGORA, ANASIL, HATALA
55 Dehn: KODER, ORUSE, DULIEL, EFINO, REDAK

14/6. Sixth Hour[56]

S	I	M	L	A	H
I	R	I	I	S	A
M	I	R	T	I	L
L	I	T	R	I	M
A	S	I	I	R	I
H	A	L	M	I	S

14/7. Seventh Hour[57]

B	A	H	A	D
A	R	I	D	A
H	I	R	I	S
A	D	I	L	A
D	A	S	A	C

14/8. Eighth Hour[58]

A	N	A	N	A	N	A
N	I	C	E	R	O	N
A	C	I	S	I	R	A
N	E	S	I	S	E	N
A	R	I	S	I	C	A
N	O	R	E	C	I	N
A	N	A	N	A	N	A

Note on 14/8: The above is my best attempt to correct this square.

---

56 Dehn: SIMLAH, IRIOSA, CHIRTIL, LITRIM, ASCIRI, HALMIS
57 Dehn: BAHAD, ERIDA, HIRIS, ADILA, HASAC
58 Dehn: ANANANA, NICERON, ACIRDIRA, MEFISEM, AFISUTA, NORECNI, ANANANA

14/9. Ninth Hour[59]

B	E	R	O	M	I	M
E	P	I	L	I	S	I
R	I	S	A	R	I	M
O	L	A	G	I	R	O
M	I	R	I	F	A	R
I	S	I	R	A	D	E
M	I	M	O	R	E	B

14/10. Tenth Hour[60]

A	L	A	M	P	I	S
L	O	N	A	R	S	I
A	N	A	D	A	I	D
M	A	D	A	G	L	O
P	R	A	G	I	A	F
I	S	I	L	A	N	E
S	I	D	O	F	E	R

Note on 14/10: The above is my best attempt to correct this square.

---

59 Dehn: BEROMIM, EPILISI, RISARDIRP, OLAGIRE, MIRIFAS, ISIRADE, MEMOREB

60 Dehn: ALAMPIS, LONARSI, ANADOAD, MADAILO, PRAEGIAT, ISILANE, SIDOFER

14/11. Eleventh Hour[61]

T	A	M	A	N
A	P	A	F	E
M	A	B	E	D
A	F	E	D	E
N	E	D	E	K

14/12. Twelfth Hour[62]

T	A	L	A	L
A	P	O	K	A
L	O	B	O	L
A	K	O	P	A
L	A	L	A	T

---

61 Dehn: TAMARE, APAFE, MABED, AFEDE, NEDAK
62 Dehn: TALAL, APOKA, LOBOL, AKORA, LALAT

Chapter Fifteen:

That the Spirits Bring All Sorts of Food and Drink

15/1. Wine[63]

I	A	I	I	N
A	R	N	A	I
I	N	O	K	I
I	A	K	L	A
N	I	I	A	I

Note on 15/1: Mathers' note was helpful here.
This square was mis-labeled as "Bread",
but the Hebrew word Yayin means "wine." (See square 3.)

15/2. Meat[64]

B	A	S	A	R
A	R	O	N	A
S	O	I	O	S
A	N	O	R	A
R	A	S	A	B

---

63 Dehn: IAYN, ARNAI, INOKI, IAKLA, NYIAI
64 Dehn: BASAR, ARONO, SOIOS, ANORA, RASAB

15/3. Bread

L	E	C	H	E	M
E	N	R	I	S	E
C	R	O	B	I	H
H	I	B	O	R	C
E	S	I	R	N	E
M	E	H	C	E	L

Note on 15/1: Mathers' note was helpful here. This square was mis-labeled as "Wine", but the Hebrew word Lechem means "bread." (See square 1.)

15/4. Fish[65]

D	A	G	A	D
A	R	O	K	A
G	O	M	O	G
A	K	O	R	A
D	A	G	A	D

---

65 Dehn: DAGAD, AROKA, GAMAG, AZORA, DAGAD

15/5. Cheese[66]

G	E	B	H	I	N	A	H
E	R	A	I	N	I	S	A
B	A	R	D	I	T	I	N
H	I	D	O	S	I	N	I
I	N	I	S	O	D	I	H
N	I	T	I	D	R	A	B
A	S	I	N	I	A	R	E
H	A	N	I	H	B	E	G

Note on 15/5: The above is my best attempt to correct this square.

---

66 Dehn: GEBHINA, ERAINISA, BARBITIN, HIDOPIRINI, INSODIH, NIDIDOAB, ASINARE, HAINHBEG

Chapter Sixteen: To Recover Treasures

16/1. Jewelery[67]

T	I	P	H	A	R	A	H
I	N	R	A	L	I	S	A
P	R	E	R	U	S	I	R
H	A	R	O	S	U	L	A
A	L	U	S	O	R	A	H
R	I	S	U	R	E	R	P
A	S	I	L	A	R	N	I
H	A	R	A	H	P	I	T

16/2. Silver[68]

C	E	S	E	P
E	L	A	T	E
S	A	R	I	S
E	T	I	K	E
P	E	S	E	C

Note on 16/2: Mathers' note was helpful here.
This square was mis-labeled as "Gold",
but the Hebrew word Keceph means "silver."

---

67 Dehn: TIPHARAH, INRALISA, PRERUSIR, HAROSOBA, ALUSORAH, RISUREP, AFILARNI, HARAPIT
68 Dehn: CESEP, ELATE, SARIS, ETIKE, PESIE

16/3. Necklaces[69]

K	A	N	A
A	L	I	G
N	I	L	I
A	G	I	S

Note on 16/3: This square appears to have been upside down.

16/4. Jewels[70]

E	B	E	N	I	E	K	A	R	A	H
B	A	L	I	O	L	A	R	E	I	A
E	L	A	A	L	O	B	B	A	I	R
N	I	A	P	I	N	E	L	N	U	A
I	O	L	I	R	I	N	I	O	E	K
E	L	O	N	I	M	I	N	O	L	E
K	A	B	E	N	I	N	A	L	O	I
A	R	B	L	I	N	A	R	Y	U	N
R	E	A	N	O	O	L	Y	A	B	E
A	I	I	U	E	L	O	U	B	M	B
H	A	R	A	K	E	I	N	E	B	E

Note on 16/4: The above square was very confusing. I have done my best to correct it.

---

69 Dehn: AGIS, NILI, ALIG, KANA
70 Dehn: EBEINEKARAH, BALIOLAREIA, BAAALOBBAIR, NIRPINEALANU, JEIARINIONEK, ELONIMINOLE, RABEMINALOI, ANALUNARYU, RIGNIOLAABE, ARIROLOEIMB, HARAKEINEBE

16/5. Treasures in General[71]

S	E	G	I	L	A	H
E	R	A	L	I	P	A
G	A	R	E	N	I	L
I	L	E	M	E	L	I
L	I	N	E	R	A	G
A	P	I	L	A	R	E
H	A	L	I	G	E	S

16/6. Treasures in General[72]

N	E	C	O	T
E	R	A	T	O
C	A	L	A	C
O	T	A	R	E
T	O	C	E	N

16/7. Treasures in General[73]

C	O	S	E	N
O	L	A	G	E
S	A	P	A	S
E	G	A	L	O
N	E	S	O	C

---

71 Dehn: SEGILAH, ERALIPA, GARENIL, ILEMEBI, INIERAG, APILARE, HALIGES
72 Dehn: NECOT, EROTO, CALAC, OTARE, TOCEN
73 Dehn: COSENS, OLAGE, SAPAS, EGALO, NESOE

16/8. Treasures in General[74]

O	T	S	A	R
T	O	E	R	A
S	E	M	E	S
A	R	E	O	T
R	A	S	T	O

16/9. Treasures in General[75]

G	E	N	A	T	I	S	I	M
E	R	O	S	I	M	U	T	I
N	O	N	A	T	A	R	A	S
A	S	A	M	I	N	A	R	I
T	I	T	I	T	I	T	I	T
I	M	A	N	I	R	O	G	A
S	U	R	A	T	O	T	I	N
I	T	A	R	I	G	I	S	E
M	I	S	I	T	A	N	E	G

Note on 16/9: This square was extremely damaged. I saw only slight hints that- perhaps!- the square was intended as a standard Acrostic with a palindrome central cross. However, it could also have been intended as a straightforward Double Acrostic. In the latter case, the square can not be corrected due to missing letters in the German original. Thus I have opted for the above correction.

---

74 Dehn: OTFAR, TOERA, SEMES, ARCOT, ROISTO
75 Dehn: GENATISIM, EROSIMUTI, MINATARAN, ATAMUNARI, TAGITISMI, INOOEROGU, SANAMATIA, HASIOPES, MARANTA

16/10. Riches in General

H	A	M	O	N	O	M	A	H
A	R	U	S	O	M	A	G	A
M	U	T	I	R	A	D	A	M
O	S	I	L	A	G	A	M	O
N	O	R	A	C	A	R	O	N
O	M	A	G	A	L	I	S	O
M	A	D	A	R	I	T	U	M
A	G	A	M	O	S	U	R	A
H	A	M	O	N	O	M	A	H

16/11. Coins

K	E	R	M	A
E	L	E	I	M
R	E	G	E	R
M	I	E	L	E
A	M	R	E	K

16/12. Treasure in General[76]

M	A	H	A	M	O	R	A	H
A	R	I	N	E	P	I	L	A
H	I	T	A	G	I	K	I	R
A	N	A	B	A	R	I	P	O
M	E	G	A	L	A	G	E	M
O	P	I	R	A	B	A	N	A
R	I	K	I	G	A	T	I	H
A	L	I	P	E	N	I	R	A
H	A	R	O	M	A	H	A	M

16/13. Treasure in General[77]

B	I	K	E	L	O	N
I	R	O	L	A	T	O
K	O	R	A	T	A	L
E	L	A	M	A	L	E
L	A	T	A	R	O	K
O	T	A	L	O	R	I
N	O	L	E	K	I	B

---

76 Dehn: MAHAMORAH, ARINEPILA, HITAGEKOR, ANABARIMO, MEGALOGIM, OPOROGENA, RIKIGETOH, ALIPENIRA, HAROMAHAM
77 Dehn: BIKELON, IROLATO, KORAMAK, ELAMATE, LATAROK, NOSEKIB, OTALORI

16/14. Especially Gold[78]

N	E	K	A	S	I	M
E	R	A	R	I	S	I
K	A	I	G	I	O	S
A	R	G	E	N	T	A
S	I	I	N	T	A	K
I	S	O	T	A	T	E
M	I	S	A	K	E	N

16/15. Money[79]

K	O	N	E	H
O	R	I	G	E
N	I	M	I	N
E	G	I	R	O
H	E	N	O	K

Note on 16/15: This square was mis-labeled as "Especially Gold", but the Hebrew word Qanah (QNH) means "to get, acquire, buy." (See square 17.)

---

78 Dehn: NEKASIM, ERARISI, KAIGIOS, ARGENTA, SYNTAK, ISOTATE, MISAKEN
79 Dehn: KONECH, ORIGE, NIMIN, EGIRO, HERAG

16/16. Treasure in General[80]

C	A	H	1	L
A	R	I	F	I
H	I	R	I	H
I	F	I	R	A
L	I	H	A	C

16/17. Especially Gold

S	E	G	O	R
E	R	O	T	O
G	O	L	O	G
O	T	O	R	E
R	O	G	E	S

Note on 16/17: This square was mis-labeled as "Money", but the Hebrew word Segor (SGOR) means "fine gold." (See square 15.)

16/18. Money[81]

B	E	T	I	S	E	R
E	L	O	R	A	G	E
T	O	T	O	N	I	S
I	R	O	M	E	N	I
S	A	N	E	L	I	T
E	G	I	N	I	S	E
R	E	S	I	T	E	B

---

80 Dehn: CAHIT, ARIFI, HIRIH, IFIRA, LIHAC
81 Dehn: BELTIFER, ELORAGE, TOTONIS, IROMENI, SANELIT, EGINISI, RESITEB

16/19. Jewels

T	I	M	I	N	O	S
I	G	A	L	E	P	O
M	A	R	O	M	E	N
I	L	O	S	O	L	I
N	E	M	O	R	A	M
O	P	E	L	A	G	I
S	O	N	I	M	I	T

16/20. Necklaces

R	A	B	I	H	I	D
A	R	O	P	A	T	I
B	O	R	O	M	A	H
I	P	O	L	O	P	I
H	A	M	O	R	O	B
I	T	A	P	O	R	A
D	I	H	I	B	A	R

Chapter Seventeen: Traveling in the Air

17/1. On a Ship[82]

B	A	S	H	E	F	I	N	A
A	G	I	A	M	I	R	O	N
S	I	L	M	I	S	A	R	I
H	A	M	O	F	U	S	I	F
E	M	I	F	A	F	I	M	E
F	I	S	U	F	O	M	A	H
I	R	A	S	I	M	L	I	S
N	O	R	I	M	A	I	G	A
A	N	I	F	E	H	S	A	B

17/2. On a Cloak

N	A	T	S	A
A	R	O	I	S
T	O	L	O	T
S	I	O	R	A
A	S	T	A	N

---

82 Dehn: BASHEFINA, AGIAMIRON, SILMISARI, HAMOFUSAT, EMIFATISE, SISELARIH, IRASIMLIS, NORIMAGIA, ANIFEHSAB

17/3. On a Cloud[83]

C	A	P	P	A	I	M
A	R	O	A	M	R	I
P	O	I	R	I	A	K
P	A	R	A	S	H	A
A	M	I	S	I	A	L
I	R	A	H	A	L	A
M	I	K	A	L	A	C

17/4. On a Cloud

A	N	A	N
N	A	S	A
A	S	A	N
N	A	N	A

17/5. On a Stick[84]

C	I	L	I	C	E	T
I	S	A	R	A	G	E
L	A	R	M	I	L	C
I	R	M	I	N	O	I
C	A	I	N	G	A	L
E	G	L	O	A	P	I
T	E	C	I	L	I	C

---

83 Dehn: CAPPAIM, AROAMRI, PLIORAK, PARASHA, ASIFIAL, IRAHALA, MIKALAC
84 Dehn: CILICET, ISARAGE, LARMILE, IRMINORI, CAINGAL, EGLOAPI, TECILU

17/6. On a Wagon[85]

A	G	A	L	A	K
G	I	D	O	K	A
A	D	I	M	A	L
L	O	M	I	O	L
A	K	A	O	M	A
K	A	L	L	A	H

---

85 Dehn: AGALAK, GIDOKA, ADIMAL, LOMIOL, AKAOMA, KAILAH

Chapter Eighteen: Healing Sicknesses

18/1. Leprosy

T	S	A	R	A	A	H
S	I	R	A	P	L	A
A	R	A	M	S	O	H
R	A	M	I	U	S	A
A	P	S	U	P	I	H
A	L	O	S	I	T	A
H	A	H	A	H	A	H

18/2. Leprosy[86]

M	E	T	S	O	R	A	H
E	L	M	I	N	I	M	A
T	M	A	R	T	M	A	R
S	I	R	G	I	L	I	O
O	N	T	I	P	I	A	S
R	I	M	L	I	A	N	T
A	M	A	I	A	N	T	E
H	A	R	O	S	T	E	M

---

[86] Dehn: METSORAH, ELMINIMA, TARTAR, SIRGILI, ONPIAS, RIMLIANT, AGAIARTE, HARSEM

18/3. Pimples and Ulcers

B	U	A	H
U	R	N	A
A	N	R	U
H	A	U	B

18/4. Plague

D	E	B	H	E	R
E	R	A	O	S	E
B	A	R	I	O	H
H	O	I	R	A	B
E	S	O	A	R	E
R	E	H	B	E	D

18/5. Stroke

S	I	T	U	K
I	R	A	P	E
T	A	R	A	H
U	P	A	L	A
K	E	H	A	H

18/6. Fever

K	A	D	A	K	A	D
A	R	A	K	A	D	A
D	A	R	E	M	A	K
A	K	E	S	E	K	A
K	A	M	E	R	A	D
A	D	A	K	A	R	A
D	A	K	A	D	A	K

18/7. Uterine Diseases[87]

R	E	C	H	E	M
E	R	H	A	S	E
C	H	A	I	A	H
H	A	I	A	H	C
E	S	A	H	R	E
M	E	H	C	E	R

18/8. Uterine Diseases[88]

B	E	T	E	N
E	M	E	R	E
T	E	N	E	T
E	R	E	M	E
N	E	T	E	B

Note on 18/8: I found the Hebrew word Beten (BTN) means "womb."

---

87 Dehn: RECHEM, ERSASE, EHARAH, HAIAHE, ESAHRE, MEHCER
88 Dehn: BELEM, EMERE, TENER, EREME, MELEB

18/9. Dizziness

R	O	K	E	A
O	G	I	R	E
K	I	L	I	K
E	R	I	G	O
A	E	K	O	R

18/10. Intestinal Colic

R	O	G	A	M	O	S
O	R	I	K	A	M	O
G	I	B	O	R	A	M
A	K	O	R	O	K	A
M	A	R	O	B	I	G
O	M	A	K	I	R	O
S	O	M	A	G	O	R

18/11. Wounds[89]

H	A	B	B	I	R
A	M	A	O	S	I
B	A	R	A	O	B
B	O	A	R	A	B
I	S	O	A	M	A
R	I	B	B	A	H

Note on 18/11: I found the Hebrew word Chabburah (ChBBURH) means "bruise, wound, blow."

---

89 Dehn: HAPPIR, AMAOSI, PARAOP, POARAP, ISOAMA, RIPPAH

Chapter Nineteen: To Achieve All Sorts of Friendships

19/1. With a Bride

C	A	L	L	A	H
A	R	I	O	T	A
L	O	R	E	I	L
L	A	M	I	E	L
A	G	N	I	P	A
H	A	L	L	A	C

19/2. With a Bridegroom

C	A	T	A	N
A	R	I	S	A
T	I	N	A	K
A	S	A	R	A
N	A	K	A	C

19/3. Courting

R	A	I	A	H
A	R	G	R	A
I	G	I	G	I
A	R	G	R	A
H	A	I	A	R

19/4. From a Particular Young Girl

D	O	D	I	M
O	B	A	L	A
D	A	R	A	C
I	L	A	P	A
M	A	C	A	R

19/5. From a Particular Judge[90]

S	I	C	O	F	E	L
I	P	E	R	I	G	E
C	E	M	A	L	I	F
O	R	A	M	A	R	O
F	I	L	A	M	E	C
E	G	I	R	E	P	I
L	E	F	O	C	I	S

19/6. From a Widow[91]

A	L	M	A	N	A	H
L	I	A	H	E	R	A
M	A	R	E	G	E	N
A	H	E	B	E	H	A
N	E	G	E	R	A	M
A	R	E	H	A	I	L
H	A	N	A	M	L	A

---

90 Dehn: SICAFEL, IPERIGE, CEMALIF, ORAMARB, FILAMEC, EGIREPI, IEFOCIS

91 Dehn: ALMANAH, LIAHERA, MAREGEN, AHEBEHA, NIGERAM, AREHAIL, HANAMLA

19/7. From a Married Woman[92]

S	I	Z	I	G	O	S
I	P	O	R	U	S	O
Z	O	L	A	F	E	G
I	R	A	G	A	M	I
G	U	F	A	P	E	Z
O	S	E	M	E	S	I
S	O	G	I	Z	I	S

19/8. From an Engaged Woman[93]

I	A	L	D	A	H
A	G	A	R	M	A
L	A	G	I	R	F
D	R	I	S	D	E
A	M	R	D	R	O
H	A	F	E	O	M

19/9. From a Particular Youth

E	L	E	M
L	A	R	E
E	R	A	L
M	E	L	E

---

92 Dehn: SIZIGOS, IPORUSO, ZOLAFEG, IRAGOMI, TURAPEZ, OZETNESR, SAGIZIS
93 Dehn: IALDACH, AGARMAH, LOGARIF, DRISE, AIRDRO, HAFEOM

19/10. From a Particular Prince[94]

N	A	G	I	D
A	K	O	R	I
G	O	L	O	G
I	R	O	K	A
D	I	G	A	N

Note on 19/10: I found the Hebrew word Nagid (NGYD) means "prince, leader, ruler, captain."

19/11. For Peace in General

S	A	L	O	M
A	R	E	P	O
L	E	M	E	L
O	P	E	R	A
M	O	L	A	S

Note on 19/11: Note the similarity of this square to the famous SATOR square.

19/12. For Friendship in General

A	H	U	B
H	A	G	E
U	G	I	E
B	E	E	Z

---

94 Dehn: MAGID, AKORI, GOLOG, IROKA, DIGAM

19/13. For the Love of a Particular Virgin

B	E	T	U	L	A	H
E	R	I	D	O	N	A
T	I	N	A	S	O	L
U	D	A	M	A	D	U
L	O	S	A	N	I	T
A	N	O	D	I	R	E
H	A	L	U	T	E	B

Note on 19/13: Mathers' note was helpful here. This square was mis-labeled as "With a Famous Man", but the Hebrew word Bethulah (BThULH) means "virgin." (See square 17.)

19/14. With a Woman[95]

I	E	D	I	D	A	T
E	R	I	D	O	N	A
D	I	L	O	G	A	H
I	D	O	L	A	C	I
D	O	G	A	R	E	B
A	N	A	C	E	R	A
T	A	H	I	B	A	T

---

95 Dehn: IEDIDAKT, ERIDONA, DILOGAH, IDOLAIB, DOGAREA, ANACERA, HATIBAT

19/15. To be Loved by a Priest[96]

S	A	Q	A	L
A	P	A	R	A
Q	A	L	A	Q
A	R	A	P	A
L	A	Q	A	S

Note on 19/15: Mathers' note was helpful here. He found that the Hebrew word Sakal (SKL) means "a wise person."

19/16. For the Love of a Lord[97]

G	E	B	H	I	R
E	R	A	I	S	A
B	A	G	O	L	I
H	I	O	L	I	A
I	S	L	I	A	H
R	A	I	A	H	A

19/17. With a Famous Man

S	A	R	A	H
A	K	E	R	A
R	E	M	E	R
A	R	E	K	A
H	A	R	A	S

Note on 19/17: Mathers' note was helpful here. This square was mis-labeled as "For the Love of a Particular Virgin", but the Hebrew word Sarah (ShRH) means "to have power." (See square 13.)

---

96 Dehn: SAGAL, APARA, GALAG, ARAPA, LAGAS
97 Dehn: GEBHIR, ERASIA, BAGOLI, HIOLIA, ISLIAH, RAIAHA

19/18. For a Particular Bridegroom[98]

C	A	T	A	N
A	R	I	S	A
T	I	N	A	K
A	S	A	R	E
N	A	K	E	L

19/19. To be Wanted and Attractive[99]

T	A	A	F	A	H
A	U	R	E	T	A
A	R	O	N	I	Z
F	E	N	A	C	A
A	T	I	C	R	O
H	A	Z	A	O	B

Note on 19/19: The above is my best attempt to correct this square.

19/20. For Adultery in General[100]

E	F	E	H	A
F	R	A	I	L
E	A	M	A	G
H	I	A	M	A
A	L	G	A	S

---

98 Dehn: CATAN, ARIFA, TINAK, ASARE, NAKEL
99 Dehn: TAAFAH, AURETA, ARONIZ, SENACA, ALIORO, THAMEB
100 Dehn: ESEHA, FROIL, CAMAG, THIAMA, ALGAS

Chapter Twenty: For All Types of Animosity

20/1. To Start Fights and Battles[101]

K	A	N	N	A
A	G	A	I	N
N	A	T	A	N
N	I	A	G	A
A	N	N	A	K

20/2. To Shoot Accurately- in General

S	E	L	A	K
E	R	A	I	A
L	A	M	A	L
A	I	A	R	E
K	A	L	E	S

20/3. To Commence Quarrels in General

A	T	L	I	T	I	S
T	R	O	M	A	L	I
L	O	G	O	S	A	T
I	M	O	R	O	M	I
T	A	S	O	G	O	L
I	L	A	M	O	R	T
S	I	T	I	L	T	A

Note on 20/3: Mathers' note was helpful here. This square was mis-labeled as "For Wrestling in General", but the Greek word Atletos means "insufferable." (See square 4.)

101Dehn: RANNA, AGAIN, NATAN, NIAGA, ANNAK

140

20/4. For Wrestling in General[102]

A	T	S	A	M	A	H
T	I	O	K	A	M	A
S	O	R	A	G	A	M
A	K	A	H	A	K	A
M	A	G	A	R	O	S
A	M	A	K	O	I	T
H	A	M	A	S	T	A

Note on 20/4: Mathers' note was helpful here. This square was mis-labeled as "To Commence Quarrels in General", but the Hebrew word Atsam means "to make strong." (See square 3.)

20/5. To Quieten the Gossip[103]

Z	O	G	E	O
O	S	O	N	E
G	O	L	O	G
E	N	O	S	O
O	E	G	O	Z

---

102 Dehn: ATSAMAH, TIOKAMA, SORAGAM, AKAHAGA, MAGAROS, AMAKOIT, HAMASTA
103 Dehn: ZOGEO, OSONE, GOLOG, ENOFO, OEGOR

20/6. To Make Enmity[104]

E	B	I	H	A	H
B	E	R	A	M	A
I	R	U	P	A	R
H	A	P	N	A	T
A	M	A	A	S	I
H	A	R	T	I	S

20/7. To Make Enmity[105]

S	I	N	A	H
I	R	A	R	A
N	A	M	I	M
A	R	I	R	A
H	A	M	A	K

Note on 20/7: The above is my best attempt to correct this square. (The author of the French manuscript made a similar attempt. See Mathers' version.) The Hebrew word Sinah (ShNAH) means "hatred."

20/8. To Make Enmity[106]

S	A	T	A	N
A	M	E	N	A
T	E	D	E	T
A	N	E	M	A
N	A	T	A	S

---

104 Dehn: EBIHAH, BERAMA, IRUPAR, HARNAT, AMAOSI, HANTIS
105 Dehn: SIMAB, IRARA, NUMIS, HAMAK, ARIRE
106 Dehn: SATAN, AMENA, TEDER, ANEMA, NATAS

20/9. Against Gossip[107]

L	O	F	I	T	O	S
O	R	A	K	I	R	O
F	A	R	O	P	I	T
I	K	O	N	O	K	I
T	I	P	O	R	A	F
O	R	I	K	A	R	O
S	O	T	I	F	O	L

20/10. To Commence War in General[108]

M	I	L	L	A	M	A
I	R	U	E	N	E	D
L	U	A	M	A	I	S
L	E	M	A	L	O	E
A	N	A	L	A	E	R
M	E	I	O	E	R	U
A	D	S	E	R	U	M

---

[107]Dehn: LOSITOS, ORAKIRO, FARAPIT, IKONOKI, FIPORAT, OSIKARO, SOTIFAL

[108]Dehn: MILLAMA, IRUENID, LIAMAIS, KEMALOE, ANALAEN, METOERI, ADSERUM

20/11. To Make Enmity[109]

M	I	G	A	B	A	H
I	R	O	D	I	S	A
G	O	N	I	M	A	B
A	D	I	S	A	K	A
B	I	M	A	N	O	G
A	S	A	K	O	L	I
H	A	B	A	G	I	M

20/12. To Make Enmity

G	I	B	O	R
I	S	E	R	E
B	E	L	E	K
O	R	E	A	K
R	E	K	K	I

20/13. To Make a Fighter Unlucky

M	A	K	I	M	O	S
A	D	I	R	A	T	E
K	I	L	O	T	E	P
I	R	O	M	E	N	A
M	A	T	E	T	O	L
O	T	E	N	O	R	A
S	E	P	A	L	A	H

---

[109]Dehn: MIGABAH, ERODISA, GONIMAB, ADISOKA, BIGANOG, SAKOLI, HABAGIM

20/14. To Make Differences Between Man and Wife[110]

G	E	B	H	I	R	A	H
E	K	L	O	A	I	R	A
B	U	A	L	G	A	A	R
H		I	S	O	P		I
I	A	G	O	R	I	A	H
R	U	I	F	I	L	I	B
A	S	U	I	T	A	M	E
H	A	R	I	H	B	E	G

Note on 20/14: This square appears to be a Double Acrostic with a Frame. I have corrected the Frame, but I can not guess at the rest of the square, or its two missing letters. I see no hint that this square should be a regular Acrostic or a 'Perfect' Double Acrostic. This appears to be the only irreparable square in the entire book.

20/15. Cause Vengeance[111]

N	E	K	A	M	A	H
E	P	A	R	A	G	A
K	A	S	O	P	I	N
A	R	O	L	A	N	I
M	A	P	A	L	O	S
A	G	I	N	O	S	E
H	A	N	I	S	E	B

---

110 Dehn: GEBHIRA, EKLOAIRA, BUALGAAR, HISOPI, FAGORIAH, RUIFILIB, ASUITAME, HARIBEG
111 Dehn: NEKAMAH, EPARAGA, HASOPIN, AROLANI, MAPOLAS, AGINOSE, HANISEB

20/16. To Make Discord and Hate Between Two Friends[112]

A	P	I	N	I	S	A
P	I	R	O	T	I	S
I	R	A	M	I	T	I
N	O	M	I	M	O	N
I	T	I	M	A	R	I
S	I	T	O	R	I	P
A	S	I	N	I	P	A

Note on 20/16: The above square was incredibly damaged. The above is my best attempt to correct it.

20/17. To Stir Up Vengeance[113]

N	A	K	A	M
A	R	O	T	A
K	O	B	A	D
A	T	A	R	O
M	A	D	O	N

Note on 20/17: This square was mis-labeled as "To Make Enmity", but the Hebrew word Naqam (NQM) means "Vengeance." (See square 19.)

---

112 Dehn: IRAMIDE, NOMINON, HIMARI, SITORIP, ASINIPA
113 Dehn: NAKAM, AROTA, KOBAD, ADARO, MADON

20/18. To Make Enmity[114]

O	H	I	E	B
H	I	A	R	E
I	A	M	A	I
E	R	A	I	H
B	E	I	H	O

20/19. To Make Enmity

K	E	L	I	M
E	G	I	S	A
L	I	R	O	K
I	S	O	G	A
M	A	K	A	N

Note on 20/19: This square was mis-labeled as "To Stir Up Vengeance", but the Hebrew word Kelimmah (KLMMH) means "disgrace, reproach, shame, insult." (See square 17.)

20/20. To Stir Up a Fight[115]

K	E	R	A	B	A	H
E	M	I	R	U	T	A
R	I	S	O	T	U	B
A	R	O	G	O	R	A
B	U	T	O	S	I	R
A	T	U	R	I	M	E
H	A	B	A	R	E	K

---

114 Dehn: OHIEB, HIARE, IAMAI, ERACH, BEIHO
115 Dehn: KERABAH, EMIRUTA, RISOTAB, AROGORA, HOLOSIR, ATURIME, HABAREK

Chapter Twenty-One: To Take on Different Appearances

21/1. Into an Old Man[116]

Z	A	K	E	N
A	C	O	G	I
K	O	L	E	M
E	G	E	R	A
N	I	M	A	S

Note on 21/1: The OT Hebrew word for "old man" is Zaqen (ZQN).

21/2. Into an Old Woman[117]

D	I	S	E	K	E	N	A	H
I	P	O	S	I	M	E	N	A
S	O	R	A	L	I	T	E	N
E	S	A	M	I	L	I	M	E
K	I	L	I	G	I	L	I	K
E	M	I	L	I	M	A	S	E
N	E	T	I	L	A	R	O	S
A	N	E	M	I	S	O	P	I
H	A	N	E	K	E	S	I	D

---

116 Dehn: ZAKEM, ACOGI, KOLEM, EGARA, MINAS
117 Dehn: DISEKENAH, IPOFIMENA, SORALILEN, ESAMILIME, GILIGILIIK, EMILIMASE, NETILAROS, ANEMISOPI, HANEKESIOL

21/3. Into a Youngster

B	A	C	U	R
A	G	O	L	U
C	O	R	O	L
U	L	O	G	A
R	U	C	A	B

21/4. Into a Young Girl[118]

I	A	L	I	D	A	H
A	R	I	P	A	S	A
L	I	G	O	Z	U	N
I	P	O	G	O	N	U
D	A	Z	O	L	I	M
A	S	U	N	I	R	E
H	A	N	U	M	E	T

Note on 21/4: This square was easy enough to correct, except for a single missing letter. The "R" in ASUNIRE is purely speculation on my part, chosen only for symmetry in the square.

21/5. Into a Boy[119]

I	O	N	E	C
O	R	A	L	E
N	A	G	A	N
E	L	A	R	O
C	E	N	O	I

---

118 Dehn: IALIDAH, ARIPASA, LIGOZUN, IPOGANU, DOZOLIM, HANUMET
119 Dehn: IONEC, ORALE, NAGAN, ELAIO, KENOI

21/6. Into a Man with a Beard[120]

D	I	S	A	K	A	N
I	R	O	G	U	L	I
S	O	L	I	G	U	M
A	G	I	L	A	S	U
K	U	G	A	R	O	A
A	L	U	S	O	A	P
N	I	M	U	A	P	A

---

120 Dehn: DISAKAN, IROGULI, SOLIGUM, AGILASU, KUGAROA, ALUSOAP, NIMIAPA

Chapter Twenty-Two: To Cause Sicknesses

22/1. Children[121]

G	E	L	A	D	I	M
E	R	A	L	A	G	I
L	A	M	O	R	U	K
A	L	O	S	O	L	A
D	A	R	O	M	I	N
I	G	U	L	I	S	A
M	I	K	A	N	A	H

Note on 22/1: The above is my best attempt to correct this square. The "H" in the lower-right corner is entirely speculation on my part. Also note this square may be mis-labeled. The OT Hebrew word Geled means "human skin" (Geledim would be the plural) Thus this square could be intended for causing skin diseases.

22/2. Farm Animals[122]

B	E	H	E	M	O	T
E	R	A	R	I	S	A
H	A	I	G	O	E	M
E	R	G	O	S	I	A
M	I	O	S	A	C	H
O	S	E	I	C	R	A
T	A	M	A	H	A	L

---

121 Dehn: GELADIM, ERALAGI, LAMORUK, OLASULA, DAMORIN, IGULISA, MIKANA
122 Dehn: BEHEMOT, ERARISA, HAIGOEM, ERGOSIA, MOISACH, OSEIARA, TANAHAL

22/3. On the Liver[123]

C	A	B	E	D
A	Z	O	T	E
B	O	R	O	B
E	T	O	Z	A
D	E	B	A	C

22/4. On the Sex Organs

M	E	B	U	S	I	M
E	R	A	G	A	L	I
B	A	R	O	N	A	S
U	G	O	G	O	G	U
S	A	N	O	R	A	B
I	L	A	G	A	R	E
M	I	S	U	B	E	M

22/5. On the Heart

L	E	B	H	A	H
E	R	O	A	S	A
B	O	K	O	A	H
H	A	O	K	O	B
A	S	A	O	R	E
H	A	H	B	E	L

---

123 Dehn: CABED, AZOTE, BOROB, ETZOA, DEBAK

22/6. On the Neck

G	A	R	A	G	A	R
A	R	I	M	A	S	A
R	I	L	O	P	A	G
A	M	O	Z	O	M	A
G	A	P	O	L	I	R
A	S	A	M	I	R	A
R	A	G	A	R	A	G

Chapter Twenty-Three: To Collapse Walls and Houses

23/1. To Collapse a House[124]

R	A	U	E	F
A	R	G	A	R
U	G	I	R	P
E	A	R	L	I
F	R	P	I	L

Note on 23/1: According to the original German, the principle word here might be RAUEH or RAUES. If the former, it could be the Hebrew word Ruk (RUQ), meaning "to make empty." The latter choice makes little sense, unless the "S" is a misprint for "F" (common in these squares), giving us RAUEF, possibly from the Hebrew word Ruph (RUPh), meaning "to shake, rock, tremble." I have chosen the latter as the more likely choice.

As a side note, the French author supposed that RAUEH should be NAUEH, which Mathers suggests is from the Hebrew word Naveh (NUH), meaning "habitation."

---

124 Dehn: RAUEH, ARGAR, UGIRP, EARLI, SIPIL

23/2. Walls[125]

C	O	M	A	H	O	N
O	S	A	R	I	N	O
M	A	E	G	R	A	L
A	R	G	I	L	I	T
H	I	R	L	A	E	P
O	N	A	I	E	R	I
N	O	L	T	P	I	H

23/3. Lift Off Roofs[126]

G	A	G	A	G
A	S	O	L	A
G	O	M	O	G
A	L	O	S	A
G	A	G	A	G

23/4. Whole Buildings[127]

B	I	N	I	A	N
I	I	N	A	S	I
N	N	I	R	A	H
I	A	R	C	A	R
A	S	A	A	T	E
N	I	H	C	E	M

Note on 23/4: The above is my best attempt to correct this square.

---

125 Dehn: COMAHON, OSARINO, NAEGRAL, ARGILIT, TIRLAEP, ONAVERI, NOLIPIH
126 Dehn: GAGAG, ASOLA, HOMOG, ALOSA, GAGAG
127 Dehn: BINIAN, NINASI, NUIRAH, IARCAR, AFOATE, NIHCEM

Chapter Twenty-Four: For the Return of Things

24/1. Jewels

K	I	K	A	L	I	S
I	R	I	N	E	G	I
K	I	N	I	M	E	L
A	N	I	D	I	N	A
L	E	M	I	N	I	K
I	G	E	N	I	R	I
S	I	L	A	K	I	K

24/2. Money[128]

G	E	N	E	B	A	K
E	R	I	K	O	N	A
N	I	R	O	F	E	H
E	K	O	R	O	K	A
B	O	F	O	R	A	B
A	N	E	K	A	S	A
K	A	H	A	B	A	R

24/3. Everything

M	O	R	E	H
O	L	O	G	E
R	O	F	O	R
E	G	O	L	O
H	E	R	O	M

---

128 Dehn: GENEBAK, ERIKONA, NIROFEH, EKOROKA, BOFORAB, ANAKASA, KALABAR

24/4. Everything[129]

F	O	N	E	F
O	R	A	T	E
N	A	G	A	N
E	T	A	R	O
F	E	N	O	F

24/5. Everything (Livestock?)

T	A	L	A	H
A	N	I	M	A
L	I	G	I	L
A	M	I	N	A
H	A	L	A	T

Note on 24/5: The French author indicates this square was for stolen or lost livestock. Probably based on the Heberw word Telah (TLH), meaning "lamb." I also find Talah (ThLH), meaning "to hang, to be hanged", though I suspect this is less likely.

---

129 Dehn: FONEF, ORATE, NAGAN, ETORO, FENOF

24/6. Everything

G	E	D	E	S	E	L	A	N
E	R	O	M	E	N	I	S	O
D	O	R	A	C	U	D	O	M
E	M	A	G	A	G	A	L	A
S	E	C	A	B	I	H	A	H
E	N	U	G	I	R	I	G	A
L	I	D	A	H	I	S	I	M
A	S	O	L	A	G	I	T	O
N	O	M	A	H	A	M	O	N

Chapter Twenty-Five:
To Stay and Move Around Under Water

25/1.

M	A	I	A	M
A	R	K	O	A
I	K	I	K	I
A	O	K	R	A
M	A	I	A	M

25/2.[130]

N	A	H	A	R	I	A	M	A
A	L	O	G	O	M	C	I	M
H	O	H	A	M	I	R	C	A
A	G	A	L	U	P	I	M	I
R	O	M	U	S	U	M	O	R
I	M	I	P	U	L	A	G	A
A	C	R	I	M	A	H	O	H
M	I	C	M	O	G	O	L	A
A	M	A	I	R	A	H	A	N

---

130 Dehn: NAHARIAMA, ALOGOMCIM, HOHAMIRCA, AGALUPIMI, ROMUSUMOR, IMIPULAGA, ACRIMAFOH, MICMOGOLA, AMAIRAHAN

Chapter Twenty-Six:
To Open and Close Locks Without a Key

26/1. Door Opening

S	A	G	A	R
A	D	O	N	A
G	O	R	O	G
A	N	O	D	A
R	A	G	A	S

26/2. Dissolving Chains

K	A	T	O	K
A	G	E	B	O
T	E	L	E	T
O	B	E	G	A
K	O	T	A	K

26/3. Opening Bolts

B	A	R	I	A	C	A
A	B	A	R	G	A	C
R	A	S	A	I	M	A
I	R	A	S	O	M	I
A	G	I	O	L	I	R
C	A	M	M	I	L	A
A	C	A	I	R	A	B

26/4. Opening Locks

S	E	G	O	R
E	L	A	F	O
G	A	S	A	G
O	F	A	L	E
R	O	G	E	S

26/5. Opening Jails

S	O	H	A	R	A	H	O	S
O	R	A	T	I	T	A	R	O
H	A	R	U	G	U	R	A	H
A	T	U	L	O	L	U	T	A
R	I	G	O	G	O	G	I	R
A	T	U	L	O	L	U	T	A
H	A	R	U	G	U	R	A	H
O	R	A	T	I	T	A	R	O
S	O	H	A	R	A	H	O	S

Chapter Twenty-Seven: To Make All Kinds of Things Appear

27/1. A Beautiful Lawn

H	E	S	E	B
E	G	A	L	E
S	A	S	A	S
E	L	A	G	E
B	E	S	E	H

27/2. A Hunting Party

K	I	N	I	G	E	S	I	A
I	R	A	S	O	G	E	T	I
N	A	G	A	R	O	S	E	S
I	S	A	L	I	T	O	G	E
G	O	R	I	L	I	R	O	G
E	G	O	T	I	L	A	S	I
S	E	S	O	R	A	G	A	N
I	T	E	G	O	S	A	R	I
A	I	S	E	G	I	N	I	K

27/3. A Gourd (Dehn: Pumpkin)[131]

K	I	K	A	I	O	N
I	L	A	P	E	N	O
K	A	L	O	S	E	I
A	P	O	K	O	P	A
I	E	S	O	L	A	K
O	N	E	P	A	L	I
N	O	I	A	K	I	K

Note on 27/3: The OT Hebrew word Qiqayon (QYQYON) means "gourd." The rest of the square is less certain. I have done my best to correct it above.

27/4. A Beautiful Garden

S	E	L	A	C
E	M	I	R	A
L	I	R	I	L
A	R	I	M	E
C	A	L	E	S

---

131 Dehn: KIKAION, ILAFENO, KALOSAI, AFOKOPA, IESOLOK, ONAPOLI, NOIAKIK

27/5. A Beautiful Palace[132]

A	T	S	A	R	A	H
T	O	A	L	I	S	A
S	A	T	O	R	I	R
A	L	O	G	O	L	A
R	I	R	O	T	A	S
A	S	I	L	A	O	T
H	A	R	A	S	T	A

27/6. A Rose Garden

R	O	D	O	N	I	A
O	R	A	G	E	S	I
D	A	L	O	P	E	N
O	G	O	L	O	G	O
N	E	P	O	L	A	D
I	S	E	G	A	R	O
A	I	N	O	D	O	R

27/7. A Big Lake[133]

A	G	A	M	A	G	A
G	U	L	O	S	E	G
A	L	I	R	U	S	A
M	O	R	I	R	O	M
A	S	U	R	I	L	A
G	E	S	O	L	U	G
A	G	A	M	A	G	A

---

132 Dehn: ATSARAH, TOALISA, SADORIR, ALOGILA, RIROTAS, ASILAOT, HARASTA

133 Dehn: AGAMAGA, GULOSEG, ALIRUSA, MORILEM, ASULILA, GESOLUG, AGAMAGA

27/8. A Snow

S	E	L	E	G
E	P	A	G	E
L	A	R	A	L
E	G	A	P	E
G	E	L	E	S

27/9. A Grape Plant or Grapes[134]

O	L	E	L	A	H
L	I	R	A	D	A
E	R	I	S	U	L
L	A	S	O	M	E
A	D	U	M	A	L
H	A	L	E	L	O

27/10. A Vineyard[135]

S	O	R	E	K
O	B	A	D	E
R	A	G	A	R
E	D	A	B	O
K	E	R	O	S

---

134 Dehn: OLELAH, LIRODA, ERISUL, LASOME, ADUMAL, HALELO
135 Dehn: SOREK, OBADE, RAGAR, EDALC, KEROS

27/11. Wild Animals[136]

C	A	I	O	T
A	I	G	R	O
I	G	I	L	I
O	R	L	I	A
T	O	I	A	C

27/12. Paddocks and Fields[137]

I	A	G	E	B
A	Z	E	R	E
G	E	S	E	G
E	R	E	Z	A
B	E	G	A	I

27/13. Farm Buildings

M	E	L	U	N	A	H
E	S	O	G	A	L	A
L	O	P	O	D	E	N
U	G	O	S	O	R	U
N	A	D	O	P	O	L
A	L	E	R	O	G	E
H	A	N	U	L	E	M

---

136 Dehn: CAIOT, AIGRO, IGILI, ORLIA, TOIAC
137 Dehn: JAGEB, AZERE, GESEG, EREZA, BEGAI

27/14. A Castle on a Mountain

A	K	R	O	P	O	L	I	S
K	O	I	S	A	N	I	L	I
R	I	P	O	R	A	T	I	L
O	S	O	S	U	M	A	N	O
P	A	R	U	S	U	R	A	P
O	N	A	M	U	S	O	S	O
L	I	T	A	R	O	P	I	R
I	L	I	N	A	S	I	O	K
S	I	L	O	P	O	R	K	A

27/15. A Mountain[138]

K	E	K	A	S	I	M
E	L	I	S	O	N	I
K	I	N	O	M	I	S
A	S	O	R	E	G	A
S	O	M	E	R	A	G
I	N	I	G	A	S	E
M	I	S	A	G	E	R

27/16. Flowers[139]

P	E	R	A	C
E	G	A	S	A
R	A	M	A	R
A	S	A	G	E
C	A	R	E	P

---

138 Dehn: KEKASIM, ELISONI, CINOMIS, ASOREGA, SOMERAG, INIGASE, MISAGER
139 Dehn: RERAC, EGASA, RAMAR, ASAGE, CAREP

27/17. Bridges

D	O	B	E	R	A	H
O	R	A	K	I	N	A
B	A	L	A	S	I	R
E	K	A	L	A	K	E
R	I	S	A	L	A	B
A	N	I	K	A	R	O
H	A	R	E	B	O	D

27/18. A Running Spring

M	A	K	O	R
A	R	I	D	O
K	I	L	I	K
O	D	I	R	A
R	O	K	A	M

27/19. A Village[140]

M	I	G	I	R	A	S
I	R	A	P	I	N	A
G	A	D	O	M	I	R
I	P	O	K	O	P	I
R	I	M	O	D	A	G
A	N	I	P	A	R	I
S	A	R	I	G	I	M

Note on 27/19: The above is my best attempt to correct this square.

---

140 Dehn: MIGIRAS, IROPENA, GADAMIR, IPAKOLI, RIMODAG, ANELORI, SARIGIM

27/20. All Sorts of Trees, or a Forest

E	S	A	H	E	L
S	U	R	O	D	E
A	R	I	L	O	H
H	O	L	I	R	A
E	D	O	R	U	S
L	E	H	A	S	E

27/21. A Lion

A	R	I	E	H
R	A	B	U	E
I	B	O	L	I
E	U	L	I	R
H	E	I	R	A

27/22. A Wild Cat[141]

L	I	N	I	R	O	S
I	P	A	S	A	L	O
N	A	C	A	M	A	R
I	S	A	G	A	S	I
R	A	M	A	C	A	N
O	L	A	S	A	P	I
S	O	R	I	N	I	L

---

141 Dehn: LINIROS, IPOSALO, NOCAMAR, ISAGASI, RAMACAN, OLASAPI, SORINIL

27/23. Cranes

S	A	S	A	S
A	R	I	K	A
S	I	G	I	S
A	K	I	R	A
S	A	S	A	S

27/24. Owls

K	I	K	I	M	I	S
I	L	O	G	E	T	I
K	O	R	A	S	E	M
I	G	A	R	A	G	I
M	E	S	A	R	O	K
I	T	E	G	O	L	I
S	I	M	I	K	I	K

27/25. Steers

P	A	R	A	H
A	Z	O	F	A
R	O	M	O	R
A	F	O	Z	A
H	A	R	A	P

27/26. Giants

A	N	A	K	I	M
N	I	P	O	G	I
A	P	O	K	O	K
K	O	K	O	P	A
I	G	O	P	I	N
M	I	K	A	N	A

27/27. Horses

R	A	M	A	C
A	G	O	R	A
M	O	L	O	M
A	R	O	G	A
C	A	M	A	R

27/28. Peacocks[142]

M	I	D	I	K	O	N
I	S	O	L	O	Z	O
D	O	P	O	T	O	K
I	L	O	K	O	L	I
K	O	T	O	P	O	D
O	Z	O	L	O	S	I
N	O	K	I	D	I	M

---

142 Dehn: MIDIKON, ISOLOZO, DOPETOK, ILOKELI, KOSTOPOD, OZOLOFI, NOKIDIM

27/29. Eagles[143]

N	E	S	I	K	E	R
E	R	A	G	O	Z	E
S	A	M	A	T	O	K
I	G	A	R	A	G	I
K	O	T	A	M	A	S
E	Z	O	G	A	R	E
R	E	K	I	S	E	N

27/30. Bears[144]

D	O	B	I	H
O	P	A	D	I
B	A	L	A	B
I	D	A	P	O
H	I	B	O	D

---

143 Dehn: NESIKER, ERAGOZE, SAMATOR, IGARAGI, KOLAMAS, EZOGARE, REKISEM
144 Dehn: DOBIH, OPADI, BALAB, IDAPO, HIBAD

27/31. Buffaloes

F	U	F	A	L	O	F
U	L	A	H	E	S	O
F	A	R	O	M	A	L
A	H	O	R	O	M	A
L	E	M	O	R	I	F
O	S	A	M	I	G	U
F	O	L	A	F	U	F

Note on 27/31: I can't help but suspect this square should begin with BUFALOS. It is common in the German originals for "F" to be mistaken for "B" or "S." I haven't found the word FUFALOF in any language as of yet.

27/32. Wild Pigs[145]

C	A	D	E	S	I	N
A	T	I	L	A	T	I
D	I	M	O	N	A	S
E	L	O	M	E	G	E
S	A	N	E	M	U	D
I	T	A	G	U	T	A
N	I	S	E	D	A	R

Note on 27/32: The second "T" in ITAGUTA is purely speculation on my part.

---

145 Dehn: CADASIN, ATILATI, DIMONAS, ELOMEGE, SANEMUD, IAGUA, RISEDAR

27/33. Dragons[146]

T	A	N	I	N
A	S	E	P	I
N	E	G	E	N
I	P	E	S	A
N	I	N	A	T

27/34. Unicorn[147]

R	E	E	M
E	L	Z	E
E	Z	L	E
M	E	E	R

27/35. Vultures[148]

A	I	I	A	H
I	U	Z	E	A
I	Z	O	Z	I
A	E	Z	U	I
H	A	I	I	A

27/36. Foxes

S	U	H	A	L
U	G	O	M	A
H	O	L	O	H
A	M	O	G	U
L	A	H	U	S

---

146 Dehn: TANIN, ASEPIN, NEGEN, IPESA, NINAL
147 Dehn: REEM, ELZE, EILE, MEER
148 Dehn: AIIAH, IUZEA, IZOZI, GEZUI, RAIAH

27/37. Griffins[149]

G	I	R	I	P	E	S
I	P	A	G	O	K	E
R	A	Z	O	T	O	P
I	G	O	S	O	G	I
P	O	T	O	Z	A	R
E	K	O	G	A	P	I
S	E	P	I	R	I	G

27/38. Rabbits

A	R	N	E	B
R	I	A	M	E
N	A	G	A	N
E	M	A	I	R
B	E	N	R	A

27/39. Dogs[150]

K	E	L	E	B
E	M	A	G	E
L	A	G	A	L
E	G	A	M	E
B	E	L	E	K

Note on 27/39: The Hebrew word for "dog" is Keleb (KLB).

---

149 Dehn: GIRIPES, IPAGOKE, RAZOTAP, IGOSOGI, PALACAR, ELOGAPI, SEPIRIG
150 Dehn: KELEF, EMAGE, LAGAL, EGAME, FELEK

Chapter Twenty-Eight: For Money in Times of Trouble

28/1. Gold Coins

S	E	G	O	R
E	G	A	M	O
G	A	Z	A	G
O	M	A	G	E
R	O	G	E	S

28/2. Medium Coins

C	E	S	E	P
E	G	O	N	E
S	O	R	O	S
E	N	O	G	E
P	E	S	E	C

28/3. Ordinary Silver[151]

M	A	T	H	A
A	I	U	A	H
T	U	R	I	T
H	A	I	A	A
A	H	T	A	M

---

151 Dehn: MATHA, AINAB, TURIT, BANAI, ATHAM

28/4. Small Coins[152]

K	E	S	E	F
E	L	A	L	E
S	A	R	A	S
E	L	A	L	E
F	E	S	E	K

Note on 28/4: Dehn does not record the above square. However, it does appear in this chapter in Dresden MS 2 (see Dehn, p. 186, illustration).

The picture includes three squares, the third of which does *not* resemble number 3 above. Therefore this could be the missing fourth square. It does resemble square number 2, but this may be due to the fact that both squares are for coins. (Keceph is OT Hebrew for "silver, money, coins.")

The author of the French text seems to have made a similar assumption, as he also provided two similar squares for coins in this chapter.

---

152 Dehn: KESEF, ELILE, SARAS, ELILE, FESEK

Chapter Twenty-Nine: To Make All Sorts of People and Armor Appear

29/1. To Make a Whole Army Corps Appear

M	A	C	A	N	E	H
A	R	A	M	O	S	E
C	A	R	I	S	O	N
A	M	I	L	I	M	A
N	O	S	I	R	A	C
E	S	O	M	A	R	A
H	E	N	A	C	A	M

29/2. To Have all Kinds of Soldiers Standing, Ready to Fight

M	A	H	A	R	A	C	A	H
A	F	I	S	O	L	E	M	A
H	I	R	E	M	U	S	A	C
A	S	E	G	A	P	O	L	A
R	O	M	A	G	I	S	I	R
A	L	U	P	I	L	E	G	A
C	E	S	O	S	E	M	E	H
A	M	A	L	I	G	E	P	A
H	A	C	A	R	A	H	A	M

29/3. To Make a Siege Appear in Front of a Town[153]

M	E	T	I	S	U	R	A	H
E	R	A	G	O	N	I	S	A
T	A	R	O	T	I	S	I	R
I	G	O	M	E	D	I	N	U
S	O	T	E	R	E	T	O	S
U	N	I	D	E	M	O	G	I
R	I	S	I	T	O	R	A	T
A	S	I	N	O	G	A	R	E
H	A	R	U	S	I	T	E	M

---

153 Dehn: METISURAH, ERAGONISA, TAROTISIR, IGOMEDINU, STOERETOS, UNIDEMOGI, RISITORAT, ASINOGARE, HARUSITEN

Chapter Thirty:

To Have the Spirits Perform Music, Singing and Juggling

30/1. Music and Songs[154]

N	E	G	I	N	A	H
E	L	E	N	A	L	A
G	E	L	A	G	A	N
I	N	A	R	A	N	I
N	A	G	A	L	E	G
A	L	A	N	E	L	E
H	A	N	I	G	E	N

Note on 30/1: The above is my best attempt to correct this square, based upon the assumption it was intended as a 'Perfect' Double Acrostic. Note that the Hebrew word Neginah (NGYNH) means "music, song, mocking song."

30/2. That the Spirits Appear as Monkeys and Perform all Sorts of Strange Dances[155]

M	E	K	O	L	A	H
E	R	A	N	O	O	A
K	A	S	I	S	O	L
O	N	I	M	I	N	O
L	O	S	I	S	A	K
A	O	O	N	A	R	E
H	A	L	O	K	E	M

Note on 30/2: The above is my best attempt to correct this square.

---

154 Dehn: MEGINAH, ELINALA, GELAGON, HARAKI, NOGALEG, ATAMILE, HANIGEM
155 Dehn: MEKOLAH, ERLAMOA, KAFISOL, ONIMINO, LOSISAK, ANOMATE, HALOKEM

30/3. For all Sorts of Music From Stringed Instruments

N	I	G	I	G	I	N
I	R	O	S	O	R	I
G	O	M	I	M	O	G
I	S	I	R	I	S	I
G	O	M	I	M	O	G
I	R	O	S	O	R	I
N	I	G	I	G	I	N

30/4. That the Spirits- Appearing as Monkeys- Perform Strange Acrobatics and Juggling[156]

M	E	R	A	S	E	F
E	P	A	R	U	S	E
R	A	L	A	P	O	S
A	R	A	K	I	S	A
S	U	P	I	N	I	R
E	S	O	S	I	M	E
F	E	S	A	R	E	M

---

156 Dehn: MERASEF, EPARUSE, CALAPOS, ARAKISA, SUPINIC, ESOSIME, FESAREM

Made in the USA
Las Vegas, NV
09 May 2025